NEW DIRECTIONS FOR CHILD DEVELOPMENT

William Damon, *Brown University*
EDITOR-IN-CHIEF

S0-EDQ-547

Close Friendships in Adolescence

Brett Laursen
Florida Atlantic University

EDITOR

Number 60, Summer 1993

JOSSEY-BASS PUBLISHERS
San Francisco

CLOSE FRIENDSHIPS IN ADOLESCENCE
Brett Laursen (ed.)
New Directions for Child Development, no. 60
William Damon, Editor-in-Chief

Microfilm copies of issues and articles are available in 16mm and 35mm, as well as microfiche in 105mm, through University Microfilms Inc., 300 North Zeeb Road, Ann Arbor, Michigan 48106.

LC 85-644581   ISSN 0195-2269   ISBN 1-55542-689-1

NEW DIRECTIONS FOR CHILD DEVELOPMENT is part of The Jossey-Bass Education Series and is published quarterly by Jossey-Bass Inc., Publishers, 350 Sansome Street, San Francisco, California 94104-1310 (publication number USPS 494-090). Second-class postage paid at San Francisco, California, and at additional mailing offices. POSTMASTER: Send address changes to Jossey-Bass Inc., Publishers, 350 Sansome Street, San Francisco, California 94104-1310.

EDITORIAL CORRESPONDENCE should be sent to the Editor-in-Chief, William Damon, Department of Education, Box 1938, Brown University, Providence, Rhode Island 02912.

Cover photograph by Wernher Krutein/PHOTOVAULT © 1990.

 The paper used in this journal is acid-free and meets the strictest guidelines in the United States for recycled paper (50 percent recycled waste, including 10 percent post-consumer waste). Manufactured in the United States of America.

Contents

EDITOR'S NOTES

Although there is a sizable literature on friendship during childhood, relatively little is known about adolescent friends. There are a variety of reasons for this lacuna. The study of adolescent relationships has long been preoccupied with parent-child bonds. Indeed, theories of adolescent development, as well as research, have concentrated almost exclusively on changes within the family unit. Friendship is slighted in part because of a lack of compelling theory (see Furman, this volume). This problem is compounded by the fact that adolescent friends are inconvenient to study; not only are older subjects more mobile than children but also they have a notorious penchant for privacy. Whatever the reason for neglect, efforts to understand close friendship during adolescence are long overdue.

This volume, *Close Friendships in Adolescence,* offers both compelling discussion and innovative research on adolescent friendship. Willard W. Hartup, in Chapter One, and Wyndol Furman, in Chapter Six, provide thoughtful opening and closing commentaries on the critical issues facing investigators in this field. Hartup summarizes pertinent literature and identifies pressing problems. Furman discusses new and critical research questions in light of the studies presented here. In between, international scholars offer a wealth of insights into adolescent friendships. William M. Bukowski, Betsy Hoza, and Michel Boivin, in Chapter Two, describe initial findings that distinguish between friendship and popularity, proposing a provocative model in which friendship exerts independent and mediating effects on emotional well-being. In Chapter Three, I elaborate on research from my own laboratory that distinguishes between close peers and other adolescent relationships on the basis of conflict management. In Chapter Four, Shmuel Shulman presents one of the first studies to identify qualitative differences among adolescent friendships; his findings challenge the status quo view that friendship is a homogeneous category. In Chapter Five, Inge Seiffge-Krenke sheds new light on adolescent perceptions of desired and actual friendships. These investigators, like the discussants, offer unique theoretical and methodological advances: Their contributions truly represent new directions.

Important developmental changes have been suggested in the functions of friendships across adolescence, as greater time is spent away from adult supervision and constraints. Although changes in form are widely acknowledged, the ramifications of these new and improved peer relationships are poorly understood. What are the nature and processes of adolescent relationships with friends? How do friendships differ, from each other, from those of earlier developmental periods, and from other adolescent relationships? This volume raises as many questions as it answers. Still, the chapters point the way toward promising new insights.

This volume grew out of the symposium International Perspectives on Close Friendship, presented at the 1992 biennial meeting of the Society for Research on Adolescence in Washington, D.C. Willard Hartup, although not a participant, graciously agreed to contribute to this volume.

Finally, I express my appreciation to each of the authors and series editor-in-chief William Damon. All were unfailingly cooperative, some despite personal adversity. I also thank my secretarial staff: Mary Davidson, Cislyn Walker, and Karen Voshall.

Brett Laursen
Editor

BRETT LAURSEN is assistant professor of psychology at Florida Atlantic University. He received his Ph.D. in child psychology in 1989 from the Institute of Child Development, University of Minnesota.

Friendships represent an important context for adolescent social development. A review of the extant literature reveals that friendships of adolescents differ in several respects from those of younger children. During adolescence, three dimensions of friendship affect the course of individual development: having friends, who one's friends are, and the quality of the friendship. Still, much remains to be learned about the nature and functions of friendship during the second decade of life, and a progressive research agenda is proposed to address this lacuna.

Adolescents and Their Friends

Willard W. Hartup

Considerable evidence now shows that peer relations contribute substantially to both social and cognitive development, and to the effectiveness with which we function as adults. Indeed, the best early predictor of adult adaptation is not IQ, or school grades, or classroom behavior but rather the adequacy with which children and adolescents get along with their contemporaries (Parker and Asher, 1987). Adolescents who are generally disliked, who are aggressive and disruptive, and who cannot establish a place for themselves in the peer culture are developmentally at risk. In this chapter, the significance of adolescent friendships is examined. Questions addressed include the following: How ubiquitous are these relationships? How similar are friends? How stable are these relationships? Does having a friend make a difference in social and emotional development? New directions in research dealing with adolescents and their friends are also discussed.

Ubiquity of Friendships

Friendships can be identified among toddlers (Howes, 1989) and obtain ubiquity by middle childhood. Friendship networks or clusters are also evident in childhood and become highly significant in adolescence.

Best Friends. Most adolescents have one or two "best friends" and several "close friends" or "good friends," the exact number depending on the manner in which best friends, close friends, and good friends are identified

Support for preparation of this chapter was provided by the Rodney S. Wallace Endowment, College of Education, University of Minnesota.

and distinguished (Crockett, Losoff, and Petersen, 1984). Best friends are usually assumed by adolescents to involve mutual attraction, and almost no one admits to not having a best friend, even on anonymous questionnaires. Self-reported best friends are most numerous in early adolescence, averaging between four and five, with this number gradually declining thereafter (Reisman and Shorr, 1978). But stable, reciprocated friendships (mutual choices lasting a year or more) are rarer, characterizing only about one-third of high school students according to one account (Epstein, 1983). Friendships are thus ubiquitous in the teenage culture, although we must recognize that more individuals report that they are involved in reciprocated friendships than actually are.

Contact among best friends usually occurs on a daily basis, and, among American teenagers, these contacts consume several hours each day (Csikszentmihalyi and Larson, 1984). Fewer than 10 percent of American adolescents have no regular contact with their friends outside school. Behavior with friends varies enormously, consisting mostly of "socializing," that is, talking on the telephone (girls more than boys), hanging out, cruising, and having fun. Among adolescents in other cultures (for example, Japan), contacts among friends are not as frequent or as time-consuming as they are among American teenagers (Savin-Williams and Berndt, 1990).

Cliques and Crowds. Friendships are dyadic. Adolescents use the phrase "my friends" to refer to a superordinate entity consisting of more than one of these relationships. Actually, "my friends" refers to an aggregate that includes one's best friends, close friends, and good friends (and perhaps *their* friends as well). These aggregates, sometimes called *cliques* or *networks*, are important structural elements in the adolescent social world and are as ubiquitous as friendships (Brown, 1989). Sometimes normative pressure from a best friend is concordant with normative pressure extending across the social network, but sometimes not. For this reason, what "my friends" think is not a proxy for what "my best friend" thinks, and the research literature must be read in this light.

Larger and looser aggregates, called *crowds,* are also evident in adolescent social relations. Sometimes crowds are regarded as collections of cliques (Dunphy, 1963), sometimes as aggregations of individuals from overlapping cliques who share certain norms (Brown, 1989) such as investment in athletics (the sporties), school achievement (the debaters), or antisocial behavior (the toughs). Even though consensus is not evident concerning the best way to describe these higher-order aggregates, one point is certain: Neither friendship functioning nor social networks can be understood without reference to them.

Cliques and crowds characterize nearly all adolescent societies (at least in the West), but their specific contours very according to community, ethnic, and historical contexts. Generally, the peer pressure associated with both cliques and crowds is multidimensional (encompasses more than a single social norm) and multidirectional (encompasses both socially sanctioned and unsanctioned norms). Pressure varies, too, with age and crowd affiliation (Brown, 1989).

At present, investigators do not have very good models with which to represent the individual adolescent within a hierarchical structure consisting of dyads, cliques, and crowds. Accordingly, we rarely consider adolescent behavior simultaneously in relation to these three contexts. Friendship relations receive more attention than either cliques or crowds probably because dyadic entities seem easier to study than polyadic ones and because most adolescents seem more invested in proximal than in distal social relations. But friendships and their significance in adolescent development cannot be appreciated out of context. Moreover, significant variation among teenagers can be traced to each of these contexts separately. For example, concordance in antisocial attitudes exists between two adolescent best friends (Kandel, 1978b), but similar concordance also exists among adolescents who "hang around together" (Cairns and others, 1988; Dishion, 1990b).

Summary. Friendships are among the most prominent features of the social landscape during adolescence. Although most teenagers consider themselves to have best friends, reciprocated friendship choices are not as common as adolescents claim. What it means to "have a friend," or, conversely, to be "friendless," varies according to the method used to identify these relationships. Cliques and crowds are other features of adolescent socialization that affect the manner in which friendships function. Currently, the interconnections among friendships, clique membership, and crowd membership are not well specified.

Friendship Stability

Friendships vary considerably in their stability. Some last for a long time, others for much shorter periods.

Beginnings, Middles, and Ends. Most friendships have beginnings, middles, and ends. Relatively little is known about the progression from one "stage" to another except that tremendous variation exists across relationships. Some friendships move quickly from beginning to end, others undergo lengthy "buildups"; some are short-lived and others long-lived. These variations are well recognized but seldom studied. Friendship dissolution occurs for myriad reasons. Personal characteristics (for example, emotional difficulties) are sometimes accompanied by friendship instability or friendlessness (Rutter and Garmezy, 1983). Relationship conditions (for example, a decreased sense of "common ground" or emotional support) may lead to friendship dissolution (Bukowski, Newcomb, and Hoza, 1987). Dissimilar attitudes toward important issues in the teenage culture also dispose toward breakup. Finally, exogenous factors may bring about friendship terminations, for example, school transitions (Berndt and Hawkins, 1991) and high school graduations (Shaver, Furman, and Buhrmester,

1985). Sometimes, the breakup is foreseeable: Unstable friends (who will eventually terminate their relationships) talk more frequently about disloyalty and lack of intimacy than do stable friends; they also report fewer contacts with one another (Berndt, Hawkins, and Hoyle, 1986).

How Stable? Although some adolescent friendships terminate, most are relatively stable across time—clearly more stable than the friendships of elementary school children. Some investigators have found that both stability and reciprocity increase from early to late adolescence (Epstein, 1983), whereas others have reported that stability reaches a peak in preadolescence, increasing only a small amount thereafter (Berndt, 1982). Most adolescents in reciprocated friendships, however, report that their relationships have lasted for substantial lengths of time (Crockett, Losoff, and Petersen, 1984); various studies show that the percentage of these relationships that last at least a year ranges upward to 70 percent (Berndt, Hawkins, and Hoyle, 1986). These data suggest that adolescent friendships are far from ephemeral entities.

Since numerous conditions bring about friendship dissolution, it is not surprising to discover that friendship stability is multidetermined. For example, adolescents who have both positive attitudes about their relationships and frequent contacts prior to school transitions are likely to remain friends afterward (Berndt and Hawkins, 1991). Friendship stability thus reflects both how well the relationship "works" and whether or not the two individuals continue to spend time with one another.

Summary. Adolescent friendships are relatively stable. When they fail, friendships are terminated for both endogenous and exogenous reasons. In some instances, the common ground supporting the relationship simply dissolves; in other instances, school or family transitions lead to the termination. In most cases, the stability or instability of these relationships is determined by more than one condition.

Conditions of Friendship

Friendships are based on reciprocity and commitment between individuals who see themselves more or less as equals. In this context, reciprocity implies mutuality in orientations and feelings. But "being friends" also implies a special sensitivity and responsibility for one another; in this sense, friendships are committed or communal relationships (Clark, Mills, and Corcoran, 1989; Collins and Repinski, in press). And friends interact on an equal power base; friendships are thus egalitarian relationships. These three friendship conditions—reciprocity, commitment, and egalitarianism—are first fully understood and appreciated during the adolescent years.

Reciprocity. Among young children, friendship expectations center on common activities and concrete reciprocities. Preschool children, for example, understand that friends share food with one another, whereas this norm does not extend to those who are not friends (Birch and Billman, 1986).

Among young children, friendship expectations center on common activities and concrete reciprocities. Common activities also undergird friendship relations in middle childhood, and adolescents expect to spend time with their friends and share activities too. But between middle childhood and middle adolescence, psychological sharing (intimacy) begins to assume significance in friendship relations (Bigelow and LaGaipa, 1980).

Intimacy differentiates middle childhood from adolescence more sharply than any other aspect of friendship relations. Indeed, the emergence of a need for intimacy (sharing thoughts and feelings with someone else) has long been regarded as the social threshold of adolescence (Sullivan, 1953). Empirical studies show that comments about shared feelings and self-disclosure appear initially in descriptions of friends during the transition to adolescence and increase steadily thereafter (Berndt, 1982; Bigelow and LaGaipa, 1980; Furman and Bierman, 1984; Furman and Buhrmester, 1992). When asked, in one investigation, to describe their relationships with their best friends in terms of self-disclosure and exchange of intimate information (for example, "I know how she feels about things without her telling me"), agreement with such statements increased between the ages of eleven and seventeen among both girls and boys (Sharabany, Gershoni, and Hofman, 1981). Manifestations of intimacy showing the greatest change with age were frankness and spontaneity, knowing and sensitivity, attachment, exclusiveness, and giving and sharing. Adolescents also expect friends, more frequently than anyone else, to meet their intimacy needs (Furman and Buhrmester, 1985).

Boys and girls both recognize that girls' relationships are more intimate than boys' (Bukowski and Kramer, 1986). Girls' assessments of their friendships show greater increases in intimacy from early to late adolescence (Sharabany, Gershoni, and Hofman, 1981); they report more frequent occurrences of self-disclosure (Rivenbark, 1971) and spend more time with their friends, on average, than do boys (Wong and Csikszentmihalyi, 1991). Some researchers have suggested that these differences may be more a matter of style than substance (Buhrmester and Furman, 1987); others have reported that the differences may reflect the greater variability of intimate behavior among boys than among girls. Youniss and Smollar (1985), for example, found that most girls describe their friendships in terms of shared activities, mutual intimacy, and understanding, whereas about 40 percent of boys describe their friendships similarly. Only about 30 percent of male relationships with friends, though, were described as guarded in communication and lacking in mutual understanding. Thus, developmental changes in intimacy must be considered against a background of sex and gender.

Adolescents and their friends thus clearly interact on the basis of reciprocity. Common interests and activities are important; intimacy is expected. Friendship expectations undergo considerable change across the transition to adolescence, but whether these changes represent cognitive elaborations of one core construct such as reciprocity (Youniss, 1980), structural transformations in the child's understanding of social relationships (Selman, 1980), or increased differentiation among relationships (Berndt and Perry, 1986; Collins and Repinski, in press) is not clear. The evidence suggests, however, that reciprocity undergirds friendship relations throughout childhood and adolescence, at the same time that the specific friendship expectations of adolescents differ from those characterizing children.

Commitment. When asked to describe their best friends (or ideal friends), both younger and older adolescents almost always mention loyalty and commitment: "A friend is a person that sticks by you when all the troubles come," and "Friends don't drop you as soon as something goes wrong" (Goodnow and Burns, 1988). Commitment is also cited by adolescents as a condition for friendship, and disloyalty is commonly the reason given for termination of a friendship. Children, in contrast, seldom mention commitment in their descriptions of best friends and seldom mention commitment issues in relation to either the strengthening or weakening of these relationships (Bigelow and LaGaipa, 1980).

Relatively little is known about the origins of social commitment, but its importance is apparent in the extent to which related constructs such as genuineness, loyalty, trust, and "being real" appear among friendship expectations. Collins and Repinski (in press) suggest that trust is one condition that attracts individuals to one another and enhances commitment. But where does trust come from? Theoretically, trust can be both a determinant and an outcome of social interaction. On the one hand, an individual's consistency and sensitivity elicit attributions by others of sincerity, truthfulness, and constancy. On the other hand, trust emerges when two individuals discover through cooperation that they can depend and rely on each other according to consensual norms (Youniss, 1980; Rotenberg and Pilipenko, 1983–1984). Trust is correlated with the quality of communication existing between adolescent friends (Armsden and Greenberg, 1987), and its appearance in adolescent friendship expectations has been linked to the greater stability of friendships among adolescents than among children (Hartup, 1992). Relatively little else, however, is known about this important friendship condition.

Conflict management is salient in the commitments of adolescent friends. Conflicts between friends are recognized as inevitable, but adolescents believe that friends have a special commitment to each other in managing conflicts: "A good friend is someone you fight with, but not forever" (Goodnow and Burns, 1988). Once again, effective conflict management is more than a friendship by-product: Effective management seems to be necessary to the continuation of these relationships and to the satisfaction that one receives from them. Accordingly, adolescents use negotiation rather than power assertion in managing their disagreements with friends, an ordering that differs from the ordering of strategies employed with parents (see Laursen, this volume, Chapter Three).

Conflicts and conflict resolutions are recognized by adolescents as events that sometimes strengthen friendships (Selman, 1980), but, generally, these relationships are seen as delicate balances of exchange in which self-interest must be weighed against consideration for the other, and conflict weighed against cooperation. Conflict management also differs between friends and nonfriends among younger children; age differences have not been directly assessed except in children's understanding of rules and responsibilities in conflicts with friends (Selman, 1980).

Equality. Peer relations are generally understood by children and adolescents to be structured horizontally rather than vertically; socializing is egalitarian, in contrast to the complementary interaction that marks relations with adults (Youniss, 1980). Consequently, both school-aged children and adolescents perceive themselves as having more power in relationships with same-sex friends than in relationships with adults (Furman, 1989). At the same time, the power base existing between same-sex friends is *not* regarded as exactly equal until midadolescence. Ratings, obtained using 5-point scales ranging from "they always [have the most power]" to "I always [have the most power]," showed that ten- and thirteen-year-olds perceived themselves as having a bit *less* power than their friends, whereas exact equivalence was evidenced only among sixteen- and nineteen-year-olds. This age difference was relatively small, but significant nevertheless. These results suggest that children and younger adolescents perceive themselves as yielding to their friends more than vice versa, whereas older adolescents do not. This interpretation is consistent with earlier results showing that conformity to peer pressure generally declines across the adolescent years (Costanzo and Shaw, 1966).

Power imbalances have important implications within relationships in that strategies for conflict resolution are related directly to them. For example, Cowan, Drinkard, and MacGavin (1984) showed that preferred modes of resolving conflicts varied according to perceived differences in relative power between competitors: With friends, both children and adolescents preferred negotiation and bargaining (strategies that always predominate when competitors are equally powerful), whereas, with adults, submission was more likely (the usual strategy when one competitor perceives himself or herself to be less powerful than the other).

Summary. The main conditions that support friendships among adolescents are reciprocity, commitment, and equality. Similar conditions support friendships among younger children, but specific manifestations differ from those supporting these relationships among adolescents.

Similarities Among Friends

Friends are similar to one another in many respects. These similarities, however, occur for several reasons.

Demographic Concordances. Adolescent friends are similar in age, race, sex, and social class. Within school grades, age concordances are not especially noteworthy, but, within schools, they are very evident. Racial concordances are also strong, and more extensive in adolescence than in middle childhood (Asher, Singleton, and Taylor, 1988). Concordances in social class are relatively constant from early to late adolescence (Epstein, 1983).

The most clear-cut concordance among adolescent friends relates to sex (see Hartup, 1983). Friendships (especially best friends) are same-sex relationships virtually by definition, so cross-sex friendships are rare. Actually, cross-sex friendships, as distinguished from romantic relationships, account for only about 5 percent of friendships in early to middle adolescence. Romantic relationships, of course, become increasingly common, but the frequency of boy-girl best friendships remains about the same as in middle childhood. Only by late adolescence does this concordance decline; Epstein (1983) reported gender concordances to be a bit more than .90 between grades six and nine, falling to about .70 among high school seniors.

Behavioral Concordances. Behavioral concordances between friends are not as strong as demographic concordances but are nevertheless appreciable. Adolescents are most similar to their friends in two general areas: (1) school-related attitudes, aspirations, and achievement (Epstein, 1983; Kandel, 1978b), and (2) attitudes and behaviors that are significant in the contemporary teenage culture, such as smoking, drinking, drug use, dating, and church attendance (Kandel, 1978b; Epstein, 1983; Karweit, 1983; Urberg, Halliday-Scher, and Tolson, 1991). Personality characteristics and social attitudes are not very concordant; friends are generally dissimilar in self-esteem, sociability, and closeness to parents. Concordances in intelligence are also not strong (Kandel, 1978b).

Similarities among friends are not greatly different for boys and girls. Boys are somewhat more likely than girls to be discordant in social class (Epstein, 1983), but, otherwise, male-female differences in these concordances occur mainly in sexual activity. Among eighth-, ninth-, and tenth-grade girls (both black and white) in the United States, friends were found to be similar in sexual behavior and attitudes, even when age and antisocial attitudes were taken into account. Among boys in these same grades, however, sexual activity (especially sexual intercourse) was not strongly concordant (Billy, Rodgers, and Udry, 1984). The reasons for this sex difference are not clear, although sexual intercourse is more directly related to social reputation among girls than it is among boys. Reputational differences, together with the greater readiness of females to engage in self-disclosure, may account for this sex difference.

Homophiletic Processes. Similarities among friends derive from three main sources: demographic homophilies, selective homophilies, and mutual socialization. Certain similarities result, first, from the manner in which the adolescent social world is organized. Demographic forces, for example, determine the segregation of neighborhoods and schools by social class and race, attitudes and abilities, norms and values. Schools are also age-graded. These demographic realities mean that adolescents have more opportunities for contact with other adolescents who are similar rather than dissimilar to themselves in age, sex, race, and social class. But social class concordances in friendship choice are somewhat reduced when schools are "highly participatory" (that is, when students all know one another and engage in many different activities) (Epstein, 1983). Racial concordances are also somewhat reduced in desegregated as compared to segregated schools (Schofield, 1982).

Similarities among friends also derive from the well-known human tendency for choosing close associates who resemble oneself (Berscheid and Walster, 1969). Socializing with a similar individual is more stimulating and rewarding than socializing with someone whose interests are vastly different; equity and reciprocity in social interaction are more likely; emotional support and consensual validation are more forthcoming; conflict and contention are minimized. Friends are never completely homomorphic, of course, and the importance of differences in friendship functioning should not be ignored, even though there is substantial evidence that friends are similar to one another.

Similarities among friends do not tell us whether adolescents select one another on the basis of similarity or whether they become similar through mutual socialization; cross-sectional data do not disentangle selection and socialization effects. Longitudinal studies reveal, however, that similarities among friends derive from both sources. Kandel (1978a), for example, found that changes in behavior over the course of a school year (in drug use, educational aspirations, involvement in delinquency) stemmed from both selection and socialization, in approximately equal amounts. Other studies have shown that friends socialize one another in their attitudes toward school and academic achievement (Epstein, 1983), sexual behavior (Billy and Udry, 1985), and use of alcohol and cigarettes (Fisher and Baumann, 1988). Relative contributions of selection and socialization to similarities among friends, however, are not always clear in these studies. One exception is that selection seems to be more important than socialization in cigarette and alcohol use (Fisher and Baumann, 1988). Such variations mean that the relative contribution of selection and socialization to friendship relations must be estimated separately for each attribute.

Summary. Friends are notably similar in sex, age, race, and social class. Behavioral similarities are most evident in educational and other normative attitudes. Friends select one another on the basis of these similarities but also socialize one another so as to become even more similar over time.

Friendships and Social Adaptation

The significance of adolescent friendships extends beyond their ubiquity. Many investigators have argued that "having friends" amounts to a developmental imperative: Good developmental outcomes depend on having friends and keeping them, friendships furnish the individual with socialization opportunities not easily obtained elsewhere (including experiences in intimacy and conflict management), and these relationships are important in emotion regulation, in self-understanding, and in formation and functioning of subsequent relationships (including romantic relationships). Folk wisdom, however, argues that people are known by the company they keep, suggesting that one's friends may exert negative as well as positive influences. There is also considerable research evidence of these influences. Consequently, *having friends*, the *identity of one's friends*, and the *quality of one's friendships* must be regarded as different variables with different developmental implications. These dimensions in friendship relations are addressed separately in the following sections.

Having Friends. Children who are disliked by other children are at risk in general, mostly for antisocial behavior in adolescence and early adulthood and for early school leaving (Parker and Asher, 1987). Being disliked and being without friends, however, are different attributes, even though rejected children have fewer friends than do popular children (Bukowski and Hoza, 1989). Estimates vary, but between 10 percent and 20 percent of rejected children and adolescents actually have friends (Hartup, 1992).

Correlational studies demonstrate that children who have reciprocated friendships are more socially competent than are children who do not. They evidence more mature perspective taking (Jones and Bowling, 1988), enter groups more easily, engage in more cooperative play, are more sociable, and have fewer difficulties with other children (Howes, 1989). School-aged children who have been referred to guidance clinics are more likely to be friendless than are nonreferred children, and, when they have them, their friendships are less stable over time (Rutter and Garmezy, 1983). Among adolescents, those with stable friendships are more altruistic than those without them (Mannarino, 1976); self-esteem is also greater (Mannarino, 1978; Bukowski, Newcomb, and Hoza, 1987). Friendless children and adolescents, in contrast, report loneliness and depression (Asher, Hymel, and Renshaw, 1984).

Correlational results are difficult to interpret. Having friends may enhance social adaptation, but the reverse may also be true. Alternatively, being sociable and having friends may derive from a common source, such as good social relationships in early childhood. Longitudinal studies assist in disentangling these effects, and research with both children and adolescents suggests that having friends contributes constructively to social adjustment. With data collected from fourth and fifth graders over a one-year interval, Bukowski, Hoza, and Newcomb (1991) showed that having friends was causally related to self-esteem but not to the children's attributions about their own social skills. Being liked (being popular), however, was causally related to self-reports about social competence but not to self-esteem. Self-worth thus appears to depend on having friends, while self-perceptions of social competence depend on being popular. Concordantly, disturbances in self-concept and social adjustment that are generally associated with school transitions during adolescence are reduced when school changes occur in the company of good friends (Simmons, Burgeson, and Reef, 1988).

Having friends may also contribute to romantic and sexual socialization. First, "having friends" as well as "having a friend to confide in" between the ages of nine and twelve were reported significantly more often by undergraduate students who had a sexual experience in childhood *with another child* than by students who did not report an experience of this kind (Haugaard and Tilly, 1988). Since most of these friendships were same-sex and most of the sexual encounters were cross-sex, these data suggest that friendships are significant in sexual socialization. But "having friends" and "having a childhood sexual experience" may both reflect some common source of variance such as self-esteem or social attractiveness, so a causal connection between them cannot be inferred. Longitudinal data, however, show that having friends between eight and twelve years of age forecasts romantic relationships between fourteen and seventeen years of age, and having a same-sex friend between fourteen and seventeen forecasts having a romantic relationship between eighteen and twenty-three (Neeman, Hubbard, and Kojetin, 1991). Note that significant correlations occurred in only one direction; same-sex friendships forecast romantic relationships, but not the reverse. Consequently, Sullivan's (1953) notions that same-sex relationships facilitate the formation and functioning of cross-sex relationships may be correct. Whether or not friendships are stepping-stones to gay and lesbian relationships is not known.

Research data suggest, then, that having a best friend is causally linked to a good developmental outcome. Friendship quality, however, was not differentiated in the studies cited above. Most likely, in these investigations, having a friend amounted to having a *good, supportive* friend, a confounding that makes it difficult to tell whether the sheer existence of these relationships or their qualities account for the outcomes noted. Friendships are not all alike, and other studies have demonstrated that who one's friends are and what these relationships are like also determine developmental outcomes.

The Company They Keep. Similarities among adolescent friends increase over time, which suggests that the company one keeps bears directly on social adjustment. Socialization effects have been demonstrated for smoking and drinking, drug use, and delinquency, as well as for educational aspirations and achievement. Taken together, these results suggest that children and adolescents who behave more-or-less normatively contribute positively to the socialization of their friends, whereas others may contribute negatively.

Several data sets reveal these dynamics clearly: Ball (1981) reported that among teenagers in lower-ranking academic streams in British schools, many individuals contributed negatively to the school success of their friends through their disruptiveness and general disinterest in school. Friends were more positive influences in higher-ranking streams, given that they were more likely to discourage disruptive, distracting behaviors and to encourage achievement. Actually, these results highlight two friendship issues: First, friends contribute either positively or negatively to adolescent socialization. Second, societal forces (for example, streaming) frequently restrict friendship opportunities to individuals who resemble one another. As mentioned earlier, friendships derive only partly from choice: Whether two individuals become friends depends on their opportunity to meet, and which individuals meet depends on the organization of the social world.

Friendship networks as well as friendship dyads demonstrate the importance of the company that one keeps. For example, aggressiveness distinguishes children who "hang around together," beginning among boys in middle childhood and becoming evident among both sexes by early adolescence (Cairns and others, 1988). Antisocial behavior (and its more deviant forms) increases among network members who are attracted to one another originally because of shared interests in antisocial activities. Actually, antisocial adolescents originate in families in which parents do not use discipline effectively or monitor their children closely (Dishion, 1990a). Such family circumstances establish children as "troublesome," which, in turn, reduces their attractiveness to others and increases the likelihood that their friends will be antisocial (Snyder, Dishion, and Patterson, 1986). Marijuana use among adolescents also seems to derive from a causal chain that begins with poor parenting, extends to the selection of friends who engage in marijuana use and other delinquent behaviors, and then involves further socialization in deviant behavior (Kandel and Andrews, 1987). Conversely, among adolescents who are at risk for antisocial behavior, "desisting" is predicted more strongly by a turning away from antisocial friends than by any other variable (Mulvey and Aber, 1988). Network socialization among adolescent friends thus resembles "shopping" or "foraging" for companions with whom there is common ground and mutual reinforcement that will sustain the network and the normative behaviors that bind its members together (Patterson and Bank, 1989).

This "shopping" model may not apply in the same way in every circumstance. In Steinberg, Dornbusch, and Brown's (1992) investigation, the academic performance of white, African American, Asian American, and Hispanic American adolescents was studied in relation to support for achievement provided by parents and friends. Students in every group whose families and friends supported academic achievement performed better than those who received support from only one source. But cultural variations were evident in the manner in which family relations and peer pressure were correlated with achievement. Among white youngsters, "authoritative" parent-child relations (that is, firm discipline, warmth, high standards) were common, disposing the children toward friendship networks that, in turn, encouraged academic success. For reasons not completely understood, however, no correlation existed between parenting practices and network affiliation among the minority students. Dynamics differed across ethnic groups: Among Asian American students, generally strong support for achievement from friends tended to offset generally negative consequences of authoritarian parenting; among African American students, generally weak support for academic achievement from friends undermined the positive effects of authoritative parenting; and Hispanic American students suffered from a combination of both parenting and friendship influences, neither of which disposed the students toward academic achievement.

The company they keep, then, has major significance in adolescents' socialization. One's friends are determined on the basis of a synergy involving both family and peer experiences as well as the organization of the adolescent social world. Different causal models may be needed, however, to describe this synergy across different cultures and for different norms.

Friendship Qualities. Some friendships are secure and smooth-sailing; others are rocky with disagreement and contention. Some friends describe their relationships as supportive and intimate; others describe theirs as rivalrous and absent of intimacy. Qualitative differences such as these are closely related to social and emotional adjustment during the teenage years: The belief that one's friends are not supportive is associated with depression and other symptomatology, especially among girls (Compas, Slavin, Wagner, and Cannatta, 1986; Feldman, Rubenstein, and Rubin, 1988), psychological and school-related problems (Kurdek and Sinclair, 1988), negative perceptions by classmates (Berndt and Hawkins, 1991), lower self-esteem (Mannarino, 1976; McGuire and Weisz, 1982), and less favorable self-perceptions of scholastic, athletic, and social competence than found when friends are considered supportive (Perry, 1987). Adolescents who perceive their friendships as supportive are more likely to be popular and considered socially competent than are adolescents with less supportive friendships (Cauce, 1986); they are also more strongly motivated to achieve, are more involved in school, have higher achievement test scores, receive higher grades, and exhibit fewer behavioral problems (Berndt and Hawkins, 1991; Cauce, 1986).

Once again, correlational findings are difficult to interpret. Satisfying friendships, for example, may constitute rose-colored glasses through which the entire world seems beautiful, as opposed to the darker glasses constituted by unsatisfying friendships. Alternatively, supportive relationships may assist adolescents in stress management and problem solving, thereby enhancing social adjustment. Or good social relations and good social adjustment may simply both be manifestations of general sociability.

Here, too, longitudinal studies assist the disentangling of effects: Berndt and Keefe (1992) asked teenagers in the fall and the spring of a school year about positive and negative qualities in their friendships (for example, emotional support and intimacy, as well as conflicts and rivalry). School involvement and conduct were rated by both the children and their teachers; grades were also studied. Correlations between friendship quality and school adjustment were calculated separately during the fall and the spring and showed again that good friendships and good school adjustment go hand in hand. Most important, regression analyses showed that students whose friendships were most intimate and supportive in the fall became increasingly involved in school, whereas those whose friendships were marred by conflict and rivalry became more disruptive and progressively less involved in school. Qualitative features of these relationships thus forecast *changes* in school adjustment. So, while supportive friendships and good school adjustment may each reflect adolescent adaptation separately, the evidence suggests that friendship quality also directly affects academic attitudes. Whether these effects extend to areas other than school adjustment is not known; additional studies are required before more can be said about friendships and their developmental significance.

Summary. Existing evidence suggests that having friends and having supportive friends are associated with two outcome clusters: (1) feeling good about oneself, feeling socially connected, and being positive (nondepressed) in outlook, and (2) being successful in subsequent relationships, especially romantic ones. The mechanisms responsible for the correlation between having friends and behavioral outcome have not been clearly established, so the findings may mean little more than that good self-attitudes are reflected in good relationships, and vice versa. But other interpretations are plausible; for example, supportive interactions with friends probably furnish adolescents with the kind of feedback and reinforcement needed for generating self-esteem. At the same time, these transactions can serve as exemplars for other relationships, with members of both the same and the opposite sex. According to this interpretation, friendship experience contributes mainly to self-attitudes and "relationship potential" rather than to general sociability or social competence.

The company one keeps (who one's friends are) contributes to adolescent socialization, too, but mainly to the kinds of norms that one internalizes, not to self-esteem or capacities for forming and maintaining relationships. Antisocial friends are likely to be antisocial influences; prosocial friends are likely to be prosocial influences. Both antisocial and prosocial friends can thus contribute positively to social adaptation as long as friendships are supportive and smooth-running. But this state of affairs also means that adolescent friendships may be both "protective" and "risk" factors—at one and the same time.

New Directions

Current research extends beyond the interest of adolescents in their friends and beyond what they expect of them. There are at least four cutting-edge issues to which investigators need to turn their attention: models for demonstrating developmental significance, processes by which friends socialize one another, qualitative differentiation among adolescent friendships, and cultural diversity in their dynamics and implications.

Developmental Models. One of the most promising new directions in research on children and adolescents is the increased effort to understand the concatenations within families and within friendship relations that together determine the course of social and emotional development. Until recently, family relations and friendship relations were regarded as nearly separate sources of variation in developmental outcome, and friendships were believed to carry relatively little weight. New models and methods, however, are challenging these notions. On the one hand, investigators are specifying the affective and cognitive processes that tie family and friendship experiences together in adolescent development. On the other hand, investigators are examining the causal chains in which family socialization constrains friendship relations, which, in turn, affect the behavior of the individual adolescent. Research in behavioral genetics is also part of this investigative effort, since individual differences in both cooperation and aggression do not seem to be completely determined by environmental variations. Different developmental models, compared and contrasted using complex quantitative methods, are being used. The work thus far indicates that having friends, the company one keeps, and friendship quality each belong in these equations, but much more needs to be done.

Modes of Social Influence. Most theories accounting for the socialization that occurs among friends are little more than theories of conformity, that is, theories dealing with group pressures and the individual's reactions to them (Berndt and Savin-Williams, in press). Social influences among friends are seldom examined as mutual, dyadic, dynamic entities. We must give greater attention to coercion, compliance, and conflict resolution, as well as to reinforcement and support in friendship interaction, considering always that these processes are dyadically regulated and occur in a time series. Finally, we seldom recognize that friends interact within higher-order social structures in which group decision making and other group interactions occur (Berndt and Savin-Williams, in press; Hinde, 1992). We still lack good models to account for the manner in which dyadic interaction between friends is moderated by the social networks to which each individual belongs, and this deficiency must be corrected. Distinctions also must be made between social influences deriving from "my best friend" and those deriving from "my friends." Relatively little is known about this entire range of processes, and relevant studies have not yet been conducted.

Friendship Qualities. One of the most significant recent advances in research dealing with adolescent friendships is the discovery that these relationships are not all alike. Considerable progress has been made in differentiating among them. Using factor analysis, Berndt and Perry (1986) discovered that the simple differentiation of "positive" and "negative" relationship features greatly assists the study of the correlates and developmental significance of friendships, among both children and adolescents. Scales are also available for differentiating among these relationships in terms of intimacy (Sharabany, Gershoni, and Hofman, 1981) and closeness (Repinski, 1992). Distinctions have also been drawn between interdependent and disengaged relationships (Shulman, this volume). But these are preliminary refinements. Friendships vary along many other dimensions, including security, diversity, the balance of power within them, and commitment (Hinde, 1979; Hartup and Sancilio, 1986). More thorough descriptions of friendships thus remain an important research objective.

Cultural Diversity. The research community still does not fully recognize that friendship processes may vary in terms of cultural and ethnic contexts. Studies have already shown that the combined influences of families and friends on academic achievement during adolescence are different across ethnic groups (Steinberg, Dornbusch, and Brown, 1992). Whatever our progress in race relations over the past forty years in the United States, adolescent societies remain segregated; the vast majority of adolescent friendships involve youngsters of the same race. Social attraction, social influence, and the social implications of adolescent friendships may be similar across ethnic groups in some ways but are undoubtedly different in other ways. At present, what we know about friendships and their developmental significance derives mainly from studies of white children and adolescents. But now that we are aware of the central role of friendship relations in social development and adaptation, some of the newly available federal funds for normative research on minority children and adolescents should be committed to the investigation of cultural diversity.

Conclusion

Current data suggest that the developmental significance of adolescent friendships extends beyond their ubiquity. The conditions giving rise to these relationships—reciprocity, commitment, and equality—are understood differently by children and by adolescents, and the stability of these relationships varies accordingly. Recent studies indicate that three dimensions of adolescent friendships affect the course of the individual's development: having friends, who one's friends are, and the quality of the friendship. The influences of family and friends combine to determine developmental outcomes, but much remains to be learned about these synergies, especially as they are played out during adolescence. Dyadic processes, through which friends influence each other, must be better conceptualized, friendship qualities must be more precisely differentiated, and cultural differences in friendship dynamics must be better documented. The active pursuit of these objectives in the years ahead promises to be fruitful.

References

Armsden, G. C., and Greenberg, M. T. "The Inventory of Parent and Peer Attachment: Individual Differences and Their Relationship to Psychological Well-being in Adolescence." *Journal of Youth and Adolescence,* 1987, *16,* 427–454.

Asher, S. R., Hymel, S., and Renshaw, P. D. "Loneliness in Children." *Child Development,* 1984, *55,* 1456–1464.

Asher, S. R., Singleton, L. C., and Taylor, A. R. "Acceptance Versus Friendship: A Longitudinal Study of Racial Integration." Unpublished manuscript, Bureau of Educational Research, University of Illinois, 1988.

Ball, S. J. *Beachside Comprehensive.* Cambridge, England: Cambridge University Press, 1981.

Berndt, T. J. "The Features and Effects of Friendship in Early Adolescence." *Child Development,* 1982, *53,* 1447–1460.

Berndt, T. J., and Hawkins, J. A. "Effects of Friendship on Adolescents' Adjustment to Junior High School." Unpublished manuscript, Psychological Sciences, Purdue University, 1991.

Berndt, T. J., Hawkins, J. A., and Hoyle, S. G. "Changes in Friendship During a School Year: Effects on Children's and Adolescents' Impressions of Friendship and Sharing with Friends." *Child Development,* 1986, *57,* 1284–1297.

Berndt, T. J., and Keefe, K. "Friends' Influence on Adolescents' Perceptions of Themselves at School." In D. H. Schunk and J. L. Meece (eds.), *Student Perceptions in the Classroom.* Hillsdale, N.J.: Erlbaum, 1992.

Berndt, T. J., and Perry, T. B. "Children's Perceptions of Friendships as Supportive Relationships." *Developmental Psychology,* 1986, *22,* 640–648.

Berndt, T. J., and Savin-Williams, R. C. "Variations in Friendships and Peer-Group Relationships in Adolescence." In P. Tolan and B. Cohler (eds.), *Handbook of Clinical Research and Practice with Adolescents.* New York: Wiley, in press.

Berscheid, E., and Walster, E. *Interpersonal Attraction.* Reading, Mass.: Addison-Wesley, 1969.

Bigelow, B. J., and LaGaipa, J. J. "The Development of Friendship Values and Choice." In H. C. Foot, A. J. Chapman, and J. R. Smith (eds.), *Friendship and Social Relations in Children.* New York: Wiley, 1980.

Billy, J.O.G., Rodgers, J. L., and Udry, J. R. "Adolescent Sexual Behavior and Friendship Choice." *Social Forces,* 1984, *62,* 653–678.

Billy, J.O.G., and Udry, J. R. "The Influence of Male and Female Best Friends on Adolescent Sexual Behavior." *Adolescence,* 1985, *20,* 21–32.

Birch, L. L., and Billman, J. "Preschool Children's Food Sharing with Friends and Acquaintances." *Child Development,* 1986, *57,* 387–395.

Brown, B. B. "The Role of Peer Groups in Adolescents' Adjustment to Secondary School." In T. J. Berndt and G. W. Ladd (eds.), *Peer Relationships in Child Development.* New York: Wiley, 1989.

Buhrmester, D., and Furman, W. "The Development of Companionship and Intimacy." *Child Development,* 1987, *58,* 1101–1113.

Bukowski, W. M., and Hoza, B. "Popularity and Friendship: Issues in Theory, Measurement, and Outcome." In T. J. Berndt and G. W. Ladd (eds.), *Peer Relationships in Child Development.* New York: Wiley, 1989.

Bukowski, W. M., Hoza, B., and Newcomb, A. F. "Friendship, Popularity, and the 'Self' During Early Adolescence." Unpublished manuscript, Department of Psychology, Concordia University, 1991.

Bukowski, W. M., and Kramer, T. L. "Judgments of the Features of Friendship Among Early Adolescent Boys and Girls." *Journal of Early Adolescence,* 1986, *6,* 331–338.

Bukowski, W. M., Newcomb, A. F., and Hoza, B. "Friendship Conceptions Among Early Adolescents: A Longitudinal Study of Stability and Change." *Journal of Early Adolescence,* 1987, *7,* 143–152.

Cairns, R. B., Cairns, B. D., Neckerman, H. J., Gest, S., and Garieppy, J. L. "Peer Networks and Aggressive Behavior: Peer Support or Peer Rejection?" *Developmental Psychology,* 1988, *24,* 815–823.

Cauce, A. M. "Social Networks and Social Competence: Exploring the Effects of Early Adolescent Friendships." *American Journal of Community Psychology,* 1986, *14,* 607–628.

Clark, M. S., Mills, J. R., and Corcoran, D. M. "Keeping Track of Needs and Inputs of Friends and Strangers." *Personality and Social Psychology Bulletin,* 1989, *15,* 533–542.

Collins, W. A., and Repinski, D. J. "Relationships During Adolescence: Continuity and Change in Interpersonal Perspective." In R. Montemayor, G. R. Adams, and T. P. Gullotta (eds.), *Advances in Adolescent Development.* Vol. 5: *Personal Relationships During Adolescence.* Newbury Park, Calif.: Sage, in press.

Compas, B. E., Slavin, L. A., Wagner, B. M., and Cannatta, K. "Relationship of Life Events and Social Support with Psychological Dysfunction Among Adolescents." *Journal of Youth and Adolescence,* 1986, *15,* 205–221.

Costanzo, P. R., and Shaw, M. E. "Conformity as a Function of Age Level." *Child Development,* 1966, *37,* 967–975.

Cowan, G., Drinkard, J., and MacGavin, L. "The Effects of Target, Age, and Gender on Use of Power Strategies." *Journal of Personality and Social Psychology,* 1984, *47,* 1391–1398.

Crockett, L., Losoff, M., and Petersen, A. C. "Perceptions of the Peer Group and Friendship in Early Adolescence." *Journal of Early Adolescence,* 1984, *4,* 155–181.

Csikszentmihalyi, M., and Larson, R. *Being Adolescent.* New York: Basic Books, 1984.

Dishion, T. J. "The Family Ecology of Boys' Peer Relations in Middle Childhood." *Child Development,* 1990a, *61,* 874–892.

Dishion, T. J. "The Peer Context of Troublesome Child and Adolescent Behavior." In P. Leone (ed.), *Understanding Troubled and Troublesome Youth.* Newbury Park, Calif.: Sage, 1990b.

Dunphy, D. C. "The Social Structure of Urban Adolescent Peer Groups." *Sociometry,* 1963, *26,* 230–246.

Epstein, J. L. "Examining Theories of Adolescent Friendship." In J. L. Epstein and N. L. Karweit (eds.), *Friends in School.* San Diego: Academic Press, 1983.

Feldman, S. S., Rubenstein, J. L., and Rubin, C. "Depressive Affect and Restraint in Early Adolescence: Relationships with Family Structure, Family Process, and Friendship Support." *Journal of Early Adolescence,* 1988, *8,* 279–296.

Fisher, L. A., and Baumann, K. E. "Influence and Selection in the Friend-Adolescent Relationship: Findings from Studies of Adolescent Smoking and Drinking." *Journal of Applied Social Psychology,* 1988, *18,* 289–314.

Furman, W. "The Development of Children's Social Networks." In D. Belle (ed.), *Children's Social Networks and Social Supports.* New York: Wiley, 1989.

Furman, W., and Bierman, K. L. "Children's Conceptions of Friendship: A Multi-Method Study of Developmental Changes." *Developmental Psychology,* 1984, *20,* 925–931.

Furman, W., and Buhrmester, D. "Children's Perceptions of the Personal Relationships in Their Social Networks." *Developmental Psychology,* 1985, *21,* 1016–1024.

Furman, W., and Buhrmester, D. "Age and Sex Differences in Perceptions of Networks of Personal Relationships." *Child Development,* 1992, *63,* 103–115.

Goodnow, J. J., and Burns, A. *Home and School: Child's Eye View.* Sydney: Allen & Unwin, 1988.

Hartup, W. W. "Peer Relations." In E. M. Hetherington (ed.), *Handbook of Child Psychology.* Vol. 4: *Socialization, Personality, and Social Development.* New York: Wiley, 1983.

Hartup, W. W. "Friendships and Their Developmental Significance." In H. McGurk (ed.), *Childhood Social Development.* Hove, England: Erlbaum, 1992.

Hartup, W. W., and Sancilio, M. F. "Children's Friendships." In E. Schopler and G. B. Mesibov (eds.), *Social Behavior in Autism.* New York: Plenum, 1986.

Haugaard, J. J., and Tilly, C. "Characteristics Predicting Children's Responses to Sexual Encounters with Other Children." *Child Abuse and Neglect,* 1988, *12,* 209–218.

Hinde, R. A. *Towards Understanding Relationships.* London: Academic Press, 1979.

Hinde, R. A. "Developmental Psychology in the Context of Other Behavioral Sciences." *Developmental Psychology,* 1992, *28,* 1018–1029.

Howes, C. *Peer Interaction of Young Children.* Monographs of the Society for Research in Child Development, vol. 53 (serial no. 217). Chicago: University of Chicago Press, 1989.

Jones, D. C., and Bowling, B. "Preschool Friends and Affective Knowledge: A Comparison of Mutual and Unilateral Friends." Paper presented at the Conference on Human Development, Charleston, South Carolina, Mar. 1988.

Kandel, D. B. "Homophily, Selection, and Socialization in Adolescent Friendships." *American Journal of Sociology,* 1978a, *84,* 427–436.

Kandel, D. B. "Similarity in Real-life Adolescent Pairs." *Journal of Personality and Social Psychology,* 1978b, *36,* 306–312.

Kandel, D. B., and Andrews, K. "Processes of Adolescent Socialization by Parents and Peers." *International Journal of the Addictions,* 1987, *22,* 319–342.

Karweit, N. "Extracurricular Activities and Friendship Selection." In J. L. Epstein and N. Karweit (eds.), *Friends in School.* San Diego: Academic Press, 1983.

Kurdek, L. A., and Sinclair, R. J. "Adjustment of Young Adolescents in Two-Parent Nuclear, Stepfather, and Mother-Custody Families." *Journal of Consulting and Clinical Psychology,* 1988, *56,* 91–96.

McGuire, K. D., and Weisz, J. R. "Social Cognition and Behavior Correlates of Preadolescent Chumships." *Child Development,* 1982, *53,* 1478–1484.

Mannarino, A. P. "Friendship Patterns and Altruistic Behavior in Preadolescent Males." *Developmental Psychology,* 1976, *12,* 555–556.

Mannarino, A. P. "Friendship Patterns and Self-Concept Development in Preadolescent Males." *Journal of Genetic Psychology,* 1978, *133,* 105–110.

Mulvey, E. P., and Aber, M. S. "Growing Out of Delinquency: Development and Desistance." In R. Jenkins and W. Brown (eds.), *The Abandonment of Delinquent Behavior: Promoting the Turn-Around.* New York: Praeger, 1988.

Neeman, J. D., Hubbard, J., and Kojetin, B. A. "Continuity in Quality of Friendships and Romantic Relationships from Childhood to Adolescence." Poster presented at the biennial meeting of the Society for Research in Child Development, Seattle, Apr. 1991.

Parker, J. G., and Asher, S. R. "Peer Relations and Later Personal Adjustment: Are Low-Accepted Children at Risk?" *Psychological Bulletin,* 1987, *102,* 357–389.

Patterson, G. R., and Bank, L. "Some Amplifier and Dampening Mechanisms for Pathologic Processes in Families." In M. Gunnar and E. Thelen (eds.), *Minnesota Symposia on Child Psychology.* Vol. 22. Hillsdale, N.J.: Erlbaum, 1989.

Perry, T. B. "The Relation of Adolescent Self-Perceptions to Their Social Relationships." Unpublished doctoral dissertation, Department of Psychology, University of Oklahoma, 1987.

Reisman, J. M., and Shorr, S. I. "Friendship Claims and Expectations Among Children and Adults." *Child Development,* 1978, *49,* 913–916.

Repinski, D. J. "Closeness in Parent-Adolescent Relationships: Contrasting Interdependence, Emotional Tone, and a Subjective Rating." Unpublished manuscript, Institute of Child Development, University of Minnesota, 1992.

Rivenbark, W. H. "Self-Disclosure Patterns Among Adolescents." *Psychological Reports,* 1971, *28,* 35–42.

Rotenberg, K. J., and Pilipenko, T. A. "Mutuality, Temporal Consistency, and Helpfulness in Children's Trust in Peers." *Social Cognition,* 1983–1984, *2,* 235–255.

Rutter, M., and Garmezy, N. "Developmental Psychopathology." In E. M. Hetherington (ed.), *Handbook of Child Psychology.* Vol. 4: *Socialization, Social Development, and Personality.* New York: Wiley, 1983.

Savin-Williams, R. C., and Berndt, T. J. "Friendship and Peer Relations." In S. S. Feldman and G. R. Elliott (eds.), *At the Threshold: The Developing Adolescent.* Cambridge, Mass.: Harvard University Press, 1990.

Schofield, J. W. *Black and White in School: Trust, Tension, or Tolerance?* New York: Praeger, 1982.

Selman, R. L. *The Growth of Interpersonal Understanding: Developmental and Clinical Analyses.* San Diego: Academic Press, 1980.

Sharabany, R., Gershoni, R., and Hofman, J. E. "Girlfriend, Boyfriend: Age and Sex Differences in Intimate Friendship." *Developmental Psychology, 1981, 17,* 800–808.

Shaver, P., Furman, W., and Buhrmester, D. "Transition to College: Network Changes, Social Skills, and Loneliness." In S. Duck and D. Perlman (eds.), *Understanding Personal Relationships: An Interdisciplinary Approach.* London: Sage, 1985.

Simmons, R. G., Burgeson, R., and Reef, M. J. "Cumulative Change at Entry to Adolescence." In M. Gunnar and W. A. Collins (eds.), *Minnesota Symposia on Child Psychology.* Vol. 21. Hillsdale, N.J.: Erlbaum, 1988.

Snyder, J., Dishion, T. J., and Patterson, G. R. "Determinants and Consequences of Associating with Deviant Peers During Preadolescence and Adolescence." *Journal of Early Adolescence, 1986, 6,* 29–43.

Steinberg, L., Dornbusch, S. M., and Brown, B. B. "Ethnic Differences in Adolescent Achievement: An Ecological Perspective." *American Psychologist, 1992, 47,* 723–729.

Sullivan, H. S. *The Interpersonal Theory of Psychiatry.* New York: Norton, 1953.

Urberg, K. A., Halliday-Scher, K., and Tolson, J. M. "Similarity Between Adolescent Best Friends." Paper presented at the biennial meeting of the Society for Research in Child Development, Seattle, Apr. 1991.

Wong, M. M., and Csikszentmihalyi, M. "Affiliation Motivation and Daily Experience: Some Issues on Gender Differences." *Journal of Personality and Social Psychology, 1991, 60,* 154–164.

Youniss, J. *Parents and Peers in Social Development: A Piaget-Sullivan Perspective.* Chicago: University of Chicago Press, 1980.

Youniss, J., and Smollar, J. *Adolescent Relations with Mothers, Fathers, and Friends.* Chicago: University of Chicago Press, 1985.

WILLARD W. HARTUP *is professor of child psychology at the Institute of Child Development, University of Minnesota, Minneapolis.*

The authors propose that popularity and friendship are linked to different forms of adjustment and emotional well-being. A central point of their model is that friendship functions as an important mediator between popularity and loneliness in early adolescence.

Popularity, Friendship, and Emotional Adjustment During Early Adolescence

William M. Bukowski, Betsy Hoza, Michel Boivin

Early adolescence is one of the most challenging developmental periods of the life span. During this time, the nature of interpersonal relationships changes as youngsters begin to function in a vast array of new environments. As part of these changes, the establishment of healthy relations with peers and the development of a sense of emotional well-being become increasingly important. In this chapter, we bring these two aspects of early adolescent development together to show how peer relations and emotional well-being are interrelated during this developmental period. In particular, we present a model of the associations between relationships with peers and feelings of belongingness and loneliness during early adolescence.

Our first goal in this chapter is to describe the two aspects of peer relations that have received the most attention in the social-developmental literature. These two constructs are popularity and friendship. In this discussion, we point to the conceptual distinctions between these two domains of experience with peers and we propose that they may become increasingly distinct forms of experience during adolescence. We also discuss the reasons why it is important to study popularity and friendship simultaneously. Next, we indicate why popularity and friendship are expected to be related to different aspects of adjustment. In this discussion,

This chapter was written with the support of the W. T. Grant Foundation Faculty Scholars Program. Correspondence should be directed to William M. Bukowski, Department of Psychology, Concordia University, Montreal, Quebec, Canada H3G 1M8.

we draw on theory taken from the work of Harry Stack Sullivan (1953) and Robert Weiss (1974). We then evaluate our model with two samples of early adolescent boys and girls. Finally, we discuss our findings and point to future directions in this area of research.

Theoretical and Empirical Background: Peer Relations and Adjustment

Our research on the association between aspects of peer relations and emotional adjustment is embedded within the larger literature regarding the links between peer relations and adjustment. The overriding premise of our research is that relations with peers influence development. Several researchers (for example, Sullivan, 1953) have argued that peer relations during early adolescence play an important, if not essential, role in the development of several aspects of competence and well-being. A particular point of this work is that relations with peers provide experiences that cannot be found in relations with parents. Specifically, whereas parent-child relationships are defined by a hierarchy of social "unequals," peer relationships consist of interaction among "equals." As a consequence, peer relationships give early adolescents important opportunities to experience acceptance, validation, and closeness. For these reasons, Sullivan argued that peer and friendship relations in early adolescence constitute a person's first true interpersonal relationships and make a profound contribution to an early adolescent's sense of well-being.

In conjunction with this theoretical literature, there is a great deal of empirical evidence that measures of peer relations are associated with measures of adjustment (see Kupersmidt, Coie, and Dodge, 1990; Parker and Asher, 1987). Indeed, numerous studies have shown that indices of adjustment can be significantly predicted from measures of peer relations. The general conclusion from this literature is that children and adolescents who do not establish good relations with peers are more likely than other children to show behavioral and emotional problems during adulthood. The obvious question raised by these observations is, "How do relations with peers affect development and adjustment in children and adolescents?" This question is the centerpiece of our research program.

What Are the Basic Dimensions of Peer Relations? When describing the effects of peer relations, many investigators have distinguished between children's and adolescents' general experiences within the peer group and their experiences on the dyadic level with particular peers (Bukowski and Hoza, 1989; Parker and Asher, in press). The experiences at the group level fall under the heading of popularity and can be further broken down into the dimensions of *acceptance* (that is, how much a child is liked by members of the peer group) and *rejection* (that is, how much a child is disliked by members of the peer group). In contrast, the experiences at the level of the dyad fall within the domain of friendship. Two aspects of friendship have been studied: whether a person has a *mutual friendship* relation with a peer and the *qualities of the friendship relation.* That is, whereas popularity refers to a child's general experiences at the level of the group, friendship refers to dyadic experiences with specific peers. It is important to note that popularity is a *unilateral* construct in that it refers to the view of the group toward the individual, and friendship is a *bilateral* construct because it refers to the relationship between two persons.

Measuring Popularity and Friendship. Because popularity and friendship are distinct constructs, they present different measurement requirements. Moreover, each of the constructs is in itself a multidimensional phenomenon. As pointed out above, there are two fundamental dimensions of popularity, acceptance and rejection. Acceptance and rejection are typically measured with nomination procedures in which children or adolescents indicate which of their peers they regard as best friends and which peers they do not like to be with. The number of times that a child is chosen as a friend is used as an index of acceptance, whereas the number of times that the child is chosen as a disliked peer is used as the index of rejection. These variables are often combined to form two higher-order measures known as *impact* and *preference.* Impact is the sum of acceptance and rejection and is an index of a child's visibility in the group. Preference is the difference between acceptance and rejection and is a measure of a child's relative likeableness.

Another means of measuring popularity is the rating scale. With this procedure, children indicate on a rating scale how much they like each of their peers. The mean of the ratings that a child or adolescent receives from peers is used as the index of popularity. Relative to nomination procedures, one drawback to the use of a mean received liking score is that it does not provide distinct indices of acceptance and rejection. Instead, the mean received liking score is probably best thought of as a construct equivalent of the preference score derived from nomination data. The important point, however, is that regardless of whether one uses a rating scale or a nomination technique, the essential feature of a popularity measure is that it represents the view of the group toward the individual.

Measures of friendship, in contrast, must reflect the properties of the relationship between two individuals. Two measures of friendship have been widely adopted. First, as an index of whether a child has a mutual friend, investigators determine whether the child makes a reciprocated friendship choice. That is, a child is regarded as having a mutual friend if he or she chooses as a best friend a peer who in turn chooses him or her as a best friend. One could adopt a very restrictive criterion whereby the reciprocated choice must be observed with the children's first friendship selection, or one could use a more liberal criterion such as accepting any reciprocated choice regardless of whether it included first choices, second choices, and so on. The important point is that this index satisfies the definition of friendship in that it is dyadic (refers to the relationship between two people) and it refers to a child's relationship with a particular peer (a peer chosen as a best friend).

Second, investigators have recently gone beyond using just an index of whether a child has a friend by turning their attention to assessment of the qualities of these friendships. We (as well as others, for example, Parker and Asher, in press) have developed procedures for assessing the qualities of children's and adolescents' best friendships according to theoretically meaningful dimensions. In our scale (Bukowski, Hoza, and Boivin, 1992), we assess five qualities of friendship: companionship, conflict, help and aid, security, and closeness. The strategy of friendship quality measures is to obtain an index of a child's impression of his or her relationship with a best friend. These measures are dyadic and bilateral in that they focus on the properties of the relationship between two individuals.

Association Between Popularity and Friendship. A final issue regarding the distinction between popularity and friendship is whether measures of these two constructs are empirically interrelated. Because popularity and friendship are distinct constructs, it is conceivable that a child who is popular may not have a mutual friend, and that a child who is unpopular may have a friendship relation. So it would seem that we should not expect measures of popularity and friendship to be related to each other. But there are other factors that would lead us to expect measures of popularity and friendship to be intercorrelated. Specifically, it is important to recognize that in order to have a mutual friend, a child must be liked by at least one other child. More important, children who are liked by many peers have more opportunities to form friendships than do children who are liked by few peers. Based on this logic, we can expect measures of popularity and friendship to show some level of interrelationship. Moreover, although popularity and friendship are conceptually distinct, both of these constructs are nevertheless related to liking. Accordingly, it is hard to imagine that there is no association between measures of popularity and measures of friendship.

In our research on this question of the link between measures of popularity and mutual friendship, we have found moderate levels of association (Bukowski, Newcomb, and Hoza, 1992). In four samples of school-age children and early adolescents, the correlation between measures of sociometric acceptance and measures of mutual friendship ranged between .38 and .49. Because each of these measures was derived from the same data (sociometric nominations), we were concerned that these correlations may have been artificially inflated. When we considered these same associations using a rating scale measure of popularity, the observed correlations were similar to those found with the nomination-based data.

Previous research indicated that popular children have more consistent friendship relations than do unpopular boys and girls. Specifically, Bukowski and Newcomb (1984) reported that friendship selections across a variety of intervals, ranging from one month to eighteen months, were more stable among popular children than among unpopular boys and girls. Taken together, these findings led to the conclusion that in spite of the conceptual distinctions between popularity and friendship, measures of these constructs are nevertheless interrelated.

Given the association between the measures of popularity and friendship, separate examination of each construct presents obvious confounds. For example, effects associated with popularity may actually be due to the fact that highly popular children are more likely to have mutual friends than are less popular children. To avoid this problem, investigators must simultaneously consider the effects of popularity and those of friendship. Only in this way can the unique and combined effects of these variables be adequately examined.

Popularity and Friendship in Adolescence

We next consider whether the association between peer relationships and adjustment changes with age.

Age Changes in Popularity and Friendship. According to theory, research, and children's comments about their peer relations, the relative importance of popularity and friendship changes across the childhood and adolescent years. The major change across these periods is an increase in the importance of interaction at the level of the dyad. For example, Sullivan (1953) proposed that for school-age children general acceptance by peers and inclusion in the "group" are of greatest concern. Exclusion from the group, he argued, can be devastating to a child's sense of well-being. At a later age, during preadolescence and early adolescence, the emphasis on peer relations shifts to dyadic experiences and relations with best friends. Sullivan believed that during early adolescence, friendship, rather than popularity, is centrally important to the development of a positive sense of well-being and adjustment. The particular qualities of friendship that he emphasized were closeness and security.

This increased emphasis on closeness and intimacy in friendship relations is also apparent in children's and early adolescents' descriptions of their friendships and discussions of the concept of friendship. Beginning with Bigelow (1977), many investigators have found that as children grow older, they attach increasing importance to the dyadic features of peer relations (Berndt, 1986; Bukowski, Newcomb, and Hoza, 1987; Furman and Bierman, 1984). Whereas young children typically say that play and companionship are the essential features of friendship relations, preadolescence and early adolescents emphasize the role of intimacy, loyalty, trust, and closeness in relations with friends. This age-related trend appears to match the developmental shift described by Sullivan.

Research on the link between intimacy and outcome also suggests an age-related increase in the importance of friendship. Buhrmester (1990), for example, has shown that intimacy is more closely associated with feelings of affective well-being during adolescence than in prior developmental periods. These findings support the view that close friendship relations take on a new importance during early adolescence.

Friendship as a Mediator Between Popularity and Adjustment. Although the research discussed in the previous section seems to support the conclusion that popularity becomes less important for adjustment during adolescence, while friendship becomes more important, it is still difficult to argue that popularity is unrelated to adjustment in early adolescence. To the extent that popularity and friendship are conceptually and empirically linked, it is unreasonable to conclude that one of these phenomena is related to adjustment whereas the other is not.

There are at least four ways in which popularity and friendship may be related to adjustment. First, popularity and friendship may both be directly and uniquely related to adjustment. Second, popularity may be indirectly linked to adjustment via the association with friendship. That is, friendship may mediate the link between popularity and adjustment. Third, and the converse of the second alternative, popularity may be directly linked to adjustment, mediating the association between friendship and adjustment. Fourth, popularity and friendship may be associated with different aspects of adjustment. Each of these options is depicted in Figure 2.1.

The increased importance of friendship during adolescence argues against the third option stated above. Indeed, given the likely link between popularity and friendship and the increased importance of friendship during adolescence, we would expect popularity to be linked to adjustment via its association with friendship rather than the other way around. Moreover, that popular children are more likely to have friends than are unpopular children argues against the first option. Accordingly, we would expect (1) popularity to be linked to adjustment by means of the mediating effect of friendship and, perhaps, (2) popularity and friendship to be related to different forms of adjustment. Clearly, in order to understand how popularity and friendship are linked to adjustment, investigators need to examine both the direct and the indirect (mediated) associations among these variables. In the next section, we discuss the possibility that popularity and friendship are linked to different aspects of adjustment.

Popularity, Friendship, and Adjustment

In this section we address the question of whether popularity and friendship have similar effects on adjustment during early adolescence.

Figure 2.1. Four Ways in Which Popularity and Friendship May Relate to Adjustment

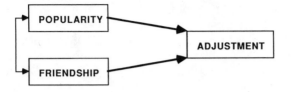

Popularity and friendship are both directly and uniquely related to adjustment.

Popularity is related to adjustment via an association with friendship.

Friendship is related to adjustment via an association with popularity.

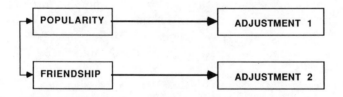

Popularity and friendship are linked to different aspects of adjustment.

Differential Links to Adjustment. To understand the contributions of popularity and friendship to development and adjustment, investigators must recognize that popularity and friendship are very different experiences. To explain the differences between the developmental significance of popularity and that of friendship, Furman and Robbins (1985) adopted the notion of "provisions," originally proposed by Weiss (1974). Provisions are the opportunities or experiences that may be available within a social or personal relationship. Furman and Robbins reasoned that popularity and friendship offer children and adolescents similar and different experiences. In particular, they reasoned that popularity offers experiences for a sense of inclusion, whereas friendship provides opportunities for loyalty, affection, and intimacy. They proposed that popularity and friendship share four provisions: help, nurturance, companionship, and enhancement of self-worth. They concluded that both popularity and friendship are important, but the two are not interchangeable.

The central point of Furman and Robbins's (1985) work is that popularity and friendship are likely to make different contributions to development. That is, although they share some provisions, popularity and friendship provide opportunities for distinct experiences.

Our position resembles an idea previously expressed by Weiss (1974). Weiss argued that different outcomes result from problems at the level of the group and the level of the dyad. Specifically, according to Weiss, when individuals are not integrated into a peer group structure, they experience feelings of social isolation; whereas when they lack an emotional closeness or exchange with chosen peers or friends, they experience feelings of "emotional loneliness." We propose that popularity, because it provides opportunities for companionship, affects early adolescents' perceptions that they "fit in" or that they are "part of the group"; whereas friendship, which provides opportunities for affectively laden experiences such as security and closeness, is related to affective aspects of adjustment, such as loneliness.

Links Among Aspects of Adjustment. A further point of our perspective is that different aspects of adjustment are interrelated. Outcome measures in many studies of peer relations are typically regarded as end points of a process. It is conceivable, however, that there is a dynamic set of associations among measures of adjustment. For example, Harter (1983) has proposed viewing the various aspects of the self-concept not as distinct end points but rather as elements of a hierarchy. In her view, perceptions of competence derive from experience and in turn influence feelings of general self-worth.

We propose a similar hierarchical model of the associations between perceptions of belongingness and feelings of loneliness. Instead of thinking of perceptions of belongingness and feelings of loneliness as separate or independent outcomes of popularity and friendship, we regard belongingness as an antecedent to feelings of loneliness. From our perspective, feelings of loneliness derive from two sources: deficiencies in relationships at the level of the dyad and perceptions of not belonging.

Multiple-Pathways Model of the Links Among Popularity, Friendship, and Adjustment in Early Adolescence

Our approach to the study of popularity, friendship, and adjustment is predicated on the following proposals: (1) Because popularity and friendship are conceptually and empirically linked to each other, they must be studied simultaneously. (2) Popularity and friendship are associated with different aspects of adjustment, namely, perceptions of belonging and feelings of loneliness, respectively. (3) During adolescence, friendship mediates the relationship between popularity and adjustment. And (4) aspects of adjustment are interrelated. The major methodological requirement of this perspective is that these measures and their interrelationships must be studied as a whole system. That is, all of the links that we identify among these measures must be examined together, including the indirect links among variables. This kind of model is not amenable to the most well known statistical tests, such as analysis of variance and multiple regression. Nevertheless, it is perfectly suited for path analysis.

Path analysis is an ideal procedure for examining our model because it produces an index of the adequacy of the whole model, indicates the strength of each individual path in the model, and assesses the direct and the indirect links among variables. The index of overall adequacy indicates whether the model provides an accurate representation of associations among variables in the model. The strengths of the particular paths in the model indicate how strongly the linked variables are associated to each other and whether each association is greater than a chance level. For the model to be accepted, coefficients for the specified links or paths must be statistically significant.

The specific model examined is depicted in Figure 2.2. In this figure, the dark arrows represent direct associations between variables: (1) Popularity (sociometric preference) is directly associated with both of the friendship measures and with perceptions of social belongingness. (2) Mutual friendship is directly linked to friendship quality, and both measures of friendship are directly associated with feelings of loneliness. (3) Social belongingness is directly linked to feelings of loneliness. Implicit in this view is the notion that popularity is related to loneliness through indirect pathways, one via mutual friendship and the other via perceptions of belongingness and inclusion.

A two-step procedure was used to assess direct and indirect links. First, the overall quality of the model was assessed with only the indirect paths among the variables of interest included, the direct links excluded. For example, the direct link between popularity and loneliness was not included in the model. In the second step, the direct links were included. (In Figure 2.2, these additional paths are indicated by gray arrows.) If the overall quality of the model is better when the new paths are included, then we conclude that this direct link is important (for example, that popularity and loneliness are linked directly). If the model does not improve, then we conclude that the association between the measures was indirect and that the direct link was not important (for example, that the association between popularity and loneliness is mediated by friendship and perceptions of belongingness). Three additional direct paths were included in our

Figure 2.2. Path Analysis Model of Links
Between Measures of Popularity and Friendship
and Measures of Social Belongingness and Loneliness

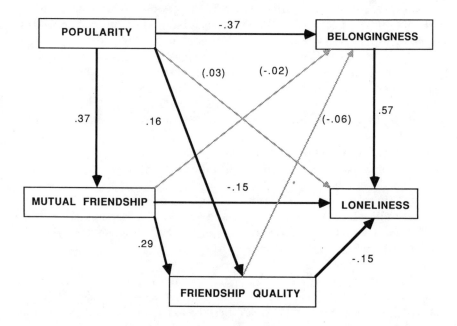

Note: All hypothesized associations in the model are represented by dark arrows. These paths are all statistically significant. The direct links, represented by gray arrows (coefficients in parentheses), are not statistically significant.

model: a link between popularity and loneliness, a link between mutual friendship and belongingness, and a link between friendship quality and belongingness.

Evaluation of the Multiple-Pathways Model

We evaluated our proposed model with a sample of 169 early adolescent boys and girls who were in grades five and six in a middle school located in the northern New England area of the United States. As part of their participation in a larger longitudinal study, these subjects completed a questionnaire on popularity, friendship and friendship quality, and loneliness and satisfaction with peer relations. Based on these data, we developed measures of popularity, mutual friendship, friendship quality, perceptions of belongingness, and feelings of loneliness. For popularity, we used a measure of sociometric preference. As noted earlier, this score is an index of a child's relative likableness in the peer group. The score is the difference between the number of times a child is chosen as a friend and the number of times the child is chosen as a disliked peer.

The mutual friendship measure indicated whether a child had a recip-rocated friend. To meet the criterion of mutual friendship, a child had to be either the first or the second choice for best friend of each of the children that he or she had chosen as a first or second best friend. Approximately half of the children in the sample met this criterion.

Friendship quality was measured with our Friendship Qualities Scale, a self-report questionnaire that we designed to assess children's impres-sions of their relationships with their best friends in terms of five dimen-sions: companionship, help or support, conflict, security, and closeness. In the current study, we focused on two of these subscales—security and closeness—because they most closely approximate the relationship provi-sions that have been identified as unique to friendship (Furman and Robbins, 1985). The items and reliability of these two subscales are shown in Table 2.1. The security subscale consists of items indicating that in times of need the child can rely on and trust his or her friend, and that if there were a quarrel or a fight or some other form of negative event in the friendship relation, the friendship would be strong enough to transcend

Table 2.1. Items in Two Subscales of the Friendship Qualities Scale

Subscale (Cronbach's alpha)	Item
Security (.73)	If I have a problem at school or at home, I can talk to my friend about it.
	If there is something bothering me, I can tell my friend about it even if it is something I cannot tell to other people.
	If I said I was sorry after I had a fight with my friend, he (she) would still stay mad at me.
	If my friend or I do something that bothers the other one of us, we can make up easily.
	If my friend and I have a fight or argument, we can say "I'm sorry" and everything will be all right.
Closeness (.79)	If my friend had to move away, I would miss him (her).
	I feel happy when I am with my friend.
	I think about my friend even when my friend is not around.
	When I do a good job at something, my friend is happy for me.
	Sometimes my friend does things for me or makes me feel special.

this problem. The items in the closeness scale focus on the sense of affection or "specialness" that the child experiences with his or her friend and the strength of the child's attachment to the friend.

To complete these two measures, subjects were asked to identify their best friends and to rate each item on a 5-point scale according to how well it described their relationships with these friends. These ratings were coded so that higher scores indicated greater levels of the quality measured.

The children in our sample also completed a scale designed by Asher, Hymel, and Renshaw (1984) to measure loneliness and social dissatisfaction. Using the subjects' ratings of the items in this scale, we tallied two scores: loneliness and social belongingness. The loneliness score was the mean of a subject's ratings of the two items in this scale that referred most directly to feelings of loneliness: "I feel alone" and "I feel lonely." The social belongingness scale included items that referred to children's feelings of inclusion and isolation: "I have lots of friends in my class," "I don't have anyone to play with," "I am well liked by the kids in my class," and "I don't have any friends in my class." The subjects rated each of these items on a 5-point scale, higher ratings indicating greater levels of loneliness and isolation from the peer group. These two scores were internally consistent (alpha = .68 and .77, for the loneliness and the social belongingness scores, respectively).

As indicated in Figure 2.2 by the dark arrows, seven paths were included in our model: popularity was linked to mutual friendship, friendship quality, and social belongingness; mutual friendship was linked to friendship quality and loneliness; and friendship quality and belongingness were linked to loneliness. We evaluated this model with Bentler's (1989) structural equations program. Our findings indicated that the model worked very well: The observed goodness-of-fit index was .91 and the chi-square value was 8.08, indicating that our model matched the data well. The path coefficients also indicated that both mutual friendship and friendship quality were linked to loneliness, and that popularity was linked to belongingness. When the model was reevaluated with direct paths between the popularity measure and the loneliness measure, the mutual friendship measure and the social belongingness measure, and the friendship quality measure and the social belongingness measure, the overall quality of the model did not improve. The coefficients for these additional paths were not statistically significant. This pattern of findings supports the argument that popularity is linked to loneliness not directly but rather indirectly via mutual friendship and feelings of belongingness.

Popularity, Friendship, and Adjustment: New Directions

Investigators who have studied the associations between peer relations and adjustment have typically focused on either a single aspect of the peer system (for example, popularity or friendship) or the additive contribution of a few variables. Although these efforts have contributed to the development of a new area of research, the researchers have failed to recognize the complex interrelatedness of constructs within the domain of peer relations. Moreover, they have not distinguished among the experiences provided by different aspects of relations with peers and thus have failed to recognize the importance of these distinctions to an understanding of how peer relations affect particular domains of adjustment.

Our approach to the study of peer relations avoids these shortcomings in four ways. First, based on what we know about the interrelatedness of popularity and friendship (and the interrelatedness of the measures used to represent these constructs), we have studied popularity and friendship simultaneously so as to avoid the confounds that result when they are studied separately.

Second, we have proposed that because popularity and friendship are different experiences, they are likely to affect different aspects of adjustment. So we have made specific hypotheses about which aspects of adjustment are linked to particular types of experience with peers. By deriving these hypotheses directly from theory about the nature of peer relations, we have been able to develop a comprehensive model of how peer relations contribute to development.

Third, both theory and research support the argument that friendship relations become increasingly important as individuals enter early adolescence. Accordingly, we have placed friendship relations at the center of our model of peer relations and adjustment. In particular, we have proposed that friendship relations are important mediators between experience at the level of the group and adjustment during early adolescence. That is, popularity and friendship are not separate pathways to affective adjustment, but friendship is the pathway by which popularity is linked to emotional adjustment. We have also proposed that popularity directly affects children's feelings of inclusion and belongingness, which in turn affect emotional well-being.

Fourth, we have considered the direct and indirect associations between measures of peer relations and measures of adjustment. Instead of looking at simple associations between measures of peer relations and measures of adjustment, we have examined how they function together. One exciting feature of this approach is the opportunity to consider the processes that link particular aspects of peer relations to adjustment. For example, our study demonstrated that friendship mediates the link between popularity and loneliness. By determining how particular variables act as mediators, we were able to identify which constructs from the peer system are directly linked to the development of affective well-being. This information not only contributes to our understanding of social and personality development but also suggests effective strategies to help early adolescents who are lonely or who lack a sense of emotional well-being.

Our findings clarify two other points as well. First, the results suggest that although children who are unpopular may not feel included in the peer group, they may nevertheless be protected from feelings of loneliness by a close and secure relationship with a best friend. In other words, the friendship relation may act as a buffer to protect unpopular children from loneliness. Second, it is important to note that mutual friendship is linked to loneliness directly and indirectly via friendship quality. That is, early adolescents who do not have a mutual friend are at risk for loneliness because they lack this kind of relationship and because nonreciprocated friendships are less likely to provide experiences for closeness and security.

Conclusion

There is a large literature demonstrating that relations with peers play an important role in social development. The goal of our research program was to identify the particular means by which peer relations and adjustment are linked during early adolescence. Our approach was predicated on the proposal that popularity and friendship constitute different forms of experience for early adolescent boys and girls, and the belief that popularity and friendship are conceptually and empirically related constructs and hence must be studied together in a unified model. By pursuing this research direction, investigators are likely to illuminate how particular domains of peer relations affect emotional adjustment during early adolescence.

References

Asher, S. R., Hymel, S., and Renshaw, P. D. "Peer Loneliness in Children." *Child Development*, 1984, *55*, 1456–1464.

Bentler, P. M. *EQS: Structural Equations Program Manual.* Los Angeles: BMDP, 1989.

Berndt, T. J. "Children's Comments About Their Friends." In M. Perlmutter (ed.), *Minnesota Symposia on Child Psychology.* Vol. 18. Hillsdale, N.J.: Erlbaum, 1986.

Bigelow, B. J. "Children's Friendship Expectations: A Cognitive-Developmental Study." *Child Development*, 1977, *48*, 247–253.

Buhrmester, D. "Intimacy of Friendship, Interpersonal Competence, and Adjustment During Preadolescence and Adolescence." *Child Development*, 1990, *61*, 1101–1111.

Bukowski, W. M., and Hoza, B. "Popularity and Friendship: Issues in Theory, Measurement, and Outcome." In T. J. Berndt and G. W. Ladd (eds.), *Peer Relationships in Child Development.* New York: Wiley, 1989.

Bukowski, W. M., Hoza, B., and Boivin, M. "The Development of a Scale to Measure Dimensions of Friendship Quality During Childhood and Early Adolescence." Unpublished manuscript, Department of Psychology, Concordia University, Montreal, 1992.

Bukowski, W. M., and Newcomb, A. F. "The Stability and Determinants of Sociometric Status and Friendship Choice: A Longitudinal Perspective." *Developmental Psychology*, 1984, *20*, 941–952.

Bukowski, W. M., Newcomb, A. F., and Hoza, B. "Friendship Conceptions Among Early Adolescents: A Longitudinal Study of Stability and Change." *Journal of Early Adolescence,* 1987, 7, 143–152.

Bukowski, W. M., Newcomb, A. F., and Hoza, B. "The Association Between Rating Scale and Nomination-Based Popularity Measures and an Index of Mutual Friendship." Unpublished manuscript, Department of Psychology, Concordia University, Montreal, 1992.

Furman, W., and Bierman, K. L. "Children's Conceptions of Friendship: A Multimethod Study of Developmental Changes." *Developmental Psychology,* 1984, 20, 925–931.

Furman, W., and Robbins, P. "What's the Point? Issues in the Selection of Treatment Objectives." In B. H. Schneider, K. H. Rubin, and J. E. Ledingham (eds.), *Children's Peer Relations: Issues in Assessment and Intervention.* New York: Springer-Verlag, 1985.

Harter, S. "Developmental Perspectives on the Self System." In E. M. Hetherington (ed.), *Handbook of Child Psychology.* Vol. 4: *Socialization, Personality, and Social Development.* New York: Wiley, 1983.

Kupersmidt, J. B., Coie, J. D., and Dodge, K. A. "The Role of Poor Peer Relations in the Development of Disorder." In S. R. Asher and J. D. Coie (eds.), *Peer Rejection in Childhood.* New York: Cambridge University Press, 1990.

Parker, J. G., and Asher, S. R. "Peer Relations and Later Personal Adjustment: Are Low-Accepted Children at Risk?" *Psychological Bulletin,* 1987, 102, 357–389.

Parker, J. G., and Asher, S. R. "Friendship and Friendship Quality in Middle Childhood: Links with Peer Group Acceptance and Feelings of Loneliness and Social Dissatisfaction." *Developmental Psychology,* in press.

Sullivan, H. S. *The Interpersonal Theory of Psychiatry.* New York: Norton, 1953.

Weiss, R. S. "The Provisions of Social Relationships." In Z. Rubin (ed.), *Doing unto Others.* Englewood Cliffs, N.J.: Prentice Hall, 1974.

WILLIAM M. BUKOWSKI is associate professor in the Department of Psychology, Concordia University, Montreal.

BETSY HOZA is assistant professor at the Western Psychiatric Institute and Clinic, Pittsburgh, Pennsylvania.

MICHEL BOIVIN is assistant professor in the School of Psychology, University of Laval, Sainte-Foy, Canada.

Unique characteristics of adolescent relationships with friends and romantic partners are evident in the resolutions and outcomes of their conflicts. New research indicates that disagreements with close peers, in contrast to those with parents and others, are managed in a manner that avoids disruption of the relationship.

Conflict Management Among Close Peers

Brett Laursen

Conflict is a ubiquitous feature in the lives of adolescents. In the course of a given day, a typical high school student participates in an average of seven disagreements with various individuals (Laursen, 1989). Indeed, children and adolescents spend more time each day engaged in conflict than in cooperation (Barker and Wright, 1955). Since conflict is an inevitable part of interactions, constructive management is a requisite skill for social competence. Children of all ages recognize that conflict can disrupt a relationship, but the awareness that successful conflict management involves a resolution satisfactory to both parties does not develop until adolescence (Selman, 1980). Although this awareness is often interpreted as evidence of a more complex understanding of interpersonal relationships, there has been little discussion of the implications that different conflict resolution strategies hold for adolescent relationships.

Interpersonal conflict is a microcosm—a brief, insightful event that reflects larger patterns of social interaction within a relationship (Collins and Laursen, 1992). Cognitive advances provide adolescents with a growing appreciation of the dangers that conflict poses to relationships (Hartup, 1992). Therefore, adolescents increasingly resolve disputes in a pragmatic, discriminating fashion, negotiating to avoid harming fragile relationships while pressing demands (when possible) in some instances and submitting (when necessary) in others.

W. Andrew Collins, Willard W. Hartup, Sarah E. Ransdell, John Ogawa, Ernest Hodges, and Amy Wilson contributed to the research described here, and their efforts are gratefully acknowledged.

This chapter is based on the premise that processes of conflict management vary as a function of the type of relationship. First, features of interpersonal conflict, defined in terms of oppositional behavior, are reviewed. Next, new research on conflict management is described. As this research indicates, adolescents interact with close peers in a manner that demonstrates awareness of the relationships' special vulnerability to disruption. Disputes with close friends and romantic partners are resolved so as to minimize the potential for negative impact, a concern that is not evident in other adolescent relationships. Finally, characteristics of adolescent relationships that mitigate conflict behavior among close peers are described.

Conflict Constructs

A state of interpersonal conflict exists when two parties disagree or are in behavioral opposition: child A influences child B, child B opposes child A (Shantz, 1987). Although some researchers argue that conflict must also include a third phase of continued opposition (child A counterprotests or resists), this more stringent criterion remains a source of debate (see Hartup and Laursen, 1993; Shantz and Hobart, 1989, for discussion). To be as inclusive as possible, the more liberal two-component, single-opposition definition is adopted for this discussion. Opposition, regardless of the number of exchanges, is the central feature of this conflict definition. The following is an example of a prototypical adolescent conflict:

ALICE: Gimme the remote control!
RALPH: No way. It's my house and I'm in charge of the remote.
ALICE: Gimme the remote control or I'm leaving.
(A sullen Ralph gives Alice the remote control.)

The conflict commences when Ralph announces his opposition to Alice's demand, and it concludes with his capitulation.

This definition explicitly distinguishes conflict from negative affect and aggression. Anger and even violence may be present during a conflict, but they need not be and often are not. The scope of conflict is not limited to fighting or arguing, and disagreements may range from the playful to the distressing.

Shantz (1987) identified a series of temporal components that together constitute a conflict: the initiation, the issue, the resolution, and the outcome. In research on adolescents, considerable attention has been focused on conflict rate differences, even though research on younger children has suggested that conflict management is a better predictor of friendship stability and individual social competence (Perry, Perry, and Kennedy, 1992). Relatively little is known about the management of adolescent conflict and the impact of these exchanges on relationships. To address this lacuna, a series of studies was conducted concerning the nature and processes of adolescent conflict with close peers.

In the research described here, two related questions were addressed: How do adolescents manage conflict with friends and romantic partners? What is the impact of conflict on these close peer relationships? The resolution and outcomes of conflicts with close peers were contrasted with conflicts arising with parents and with other adults and peers. First, a meta-analysis was conducted to determine whether patterns of conflict resolution distinguish close peer relationships from all other types. Second, questionnaire and telephone interview data were collected to compare conflict outcomes across various types of adolescent relationships.

Resolution of Conflict

As investigators have begun to appreciate the salience of conflict in the lives of adolescents, research on conflict resolution has multiplied. As the number of these studies increases, so too does the need for an empirical summary of the literature.

Meta-Analysis Methods. To determine styles of adolescent conflict resolution characteristic of friends and romantic partners, a meta-analysis was conducted to compare the strategies employed with close peers to those employed with parents and others. A computer search of the ERIC and PSYCHLIT data bases for the years 1974 through 1991 identified research abstracts containing the following keywords: agonism, argument, conflict, dispute, disagree, negotiate, and resolution. Four criteria were established for a study to be included in the meta-analysis: (1) subject samples consisting of adolescents ranging in age from twelve to twenty-one; (2) operational definitions of conflict consistent with Shantz's (1987) opposition construct, that is, studies were omitted if conflict was defined in terms of traits (for example, quarrelsome), competition (for example, the Prisoner's Dilemma), dominance (for example, speech interruptions), or aggression; (3) conflict, whether real or hypothetical, entailing dyadic, not intrapsychic or group, exchanges; and (4) specific styles of conflict resolution assayed within one or more adolescent relationships.

Resolutions were defined in terms of behaviors or tactics that terminated conflicts. Across studies, resolutions encompassed a variety of strategies. For the present investigation, resolutions were coded within the framework of three mutually exclusively categories: power assertion, negotiation and compromise, and disengagement (see Vuchinich, 1990; Hartup and Laursen, 1993). A study was omitted if all three resolution strategies were not represented or if categories were not mutually exclusive. Third-party resolutions were also identified but were later excluded because too few investigations examined this tactic.

Power assertion involves a process where one party persists in assertions until the other submits or capitulates. For example, in the prototypical adolescent conflict presented above, Alice continued to demand the remote control and Ralph finally gave in. Negotiation and compromise entail consensus, a middle ground between two opposing positions. If Alice had offered to share the remote control and Ralph had accepted, the two would have achieved a negotiated resolution. Disengagement describes a wide range of behaviors that terminate a dispute without achieving a solution, including standoff (dropping the conflict or changing the subject) and withdrawal (refusing to continue). For Alice and Ralph, an announcement of "dinnertime" would have probably produced disengagement.

Of the seventy-nine studies identified from abstracts, twelve met all four criteria and qualified for the meta-analysis (see Appendix). One-quarter of the studies identified from abstracts were reviewed by two coders, who achieved 100 percent agreement in identifying the studies that qualified for inclusion in the meta-analysis. Interrater agreement for coding conflict resolutions was 93 percent (kappa = .90).

For each of the twelve investigations, conflict participants were classified as close peers (friends or romantic partners), parents (mothers or fathers), or other adults and peers (teachers, employers, peers, or co-workers). Nine studies examined the resolution of conflicts between close peers, producing data for comparisons across eleven different types of close friends or romantic partners. Seven involved conflicts with parents, from which eight different parent-adolescent relationship comparisons were derived. Four included conflicts in other relationships, resulting in four different relationship comparisons encompassing teachers, employers, and peer acquaintances. Only two studies examined conflicts with siblings, too few for a separate relationship category.

For each within–relationship category comparison, three conflict resolution effect sizes were calculated: power assertion versus negotiation, power assertion versus disengagement, and negotiation versus disengagement. Effect sizes were computed from either means and standard deviations or from results of statistical tests (chi-square, t, or F values). The Pearson product-moment correlation r was selected as the common metric statistic of effect size.

Meta-Analysis Results. Separate within–relationship category comparisons of conflict resolution strategies were conducted for close peers, parents, and others (all p's < .001). Since results did not differ when weighted by sample sizes, unweighted effects are reported here. As a guideline, Cohen (1977) suggested that significant differences in correlational data be interpreted in terms of small ($r = .1$), medium ($r = .3$), and large ($r = .5$) effects.

Close peers more frequently engaged in negotiation than power assertion ($r = .19$); negotiation also prevailed over disengagement ($r = .17$). There were no significant differences in rates of close peer disengagement and power assertion. In contrast, disagreements with parents involved more power assertion than negotiation (r = .32); power assertion was also more prevalent than disengagement (r = .15). Rates of parent-adolescent disengagement were greater than negotiation (r = .23). In other relationships, levels of power assertion resembled the level with parents: Power assertion resolutions were more frequent than either disengagement (r = .21) or negotiation (r = .11). In another respect, however, these other relationships were more similar to close peers, with rates of negotiation greater than disengagement (r = .15).

Resolutions were diametrically opposed across relationship categories; adolescents' conflict management with close peers was different from that with parents and others. Close friends and romantic partners shunned power assertion and disengagement in favor of negotiation. Among interactions with parents and others, power assertion emerged as the dominant resolution strategy. Relative to close peers, adolescents reported less negotiation with parents and less disengagement with others. Figure 3.1 summarizes findings from ten of the twelve studies included in the meta-analysis. Similar results were reported in the two excluded reports, but response items (for example, "somewhat" and "very" likely to negotiate) could not be converted to percentage scores.

Additional analyses indicated considerable sample heterogeneity, suggesting the possible presence of moderator variables (Hedges and Olkin, 1985). Unfortunately, too few studies were available to examine potential interactions. The results must therefore be interpreted with caution, since conflict resolution styles within relationship categories may vary according to gender, context, and other variables.

Outcomes of Conflict

Conflicts have myriad effects on individuals and relationships. Some outcomes are short-lived and inconsequential, whereas others produce long-term changes in the participants and their future exchanges.

Questionnaire and Telephone Interview Methods. Do differences in the way close peers resolve disputes carry over into the realm of conflict outcomes? To address this question, two additional investigations were conducted, detailing conflict outcomes in adolescent relationships with close friends and romantic partners, parents, and other adults and peers. In the first, 685 high school students (ranging in age from fifteen to eighteen; M = sixteen years, seven months) completed questionnaires concerning all conflicts from the previous school day. In the second study, telephone interviews were conducted with a subsample of 143 adolescents, who described their conflicts in greater detail.

In both investigations, adolescents reviewed a list of thirty-four conflict topics adapted from the Issues Checklist (Prinz, Foster, Kent, and O'Leary, 1979; Robin and Foster, 1984). For each topic, subjects indicated whether a conflict had arisen the previous day and, if so, whom it involved. Conflict was

Figure 3.1. Mean Proportion of Conflict Resolution Strategies in Adolescent Relationships: Unweighted Meta-Analysis Results

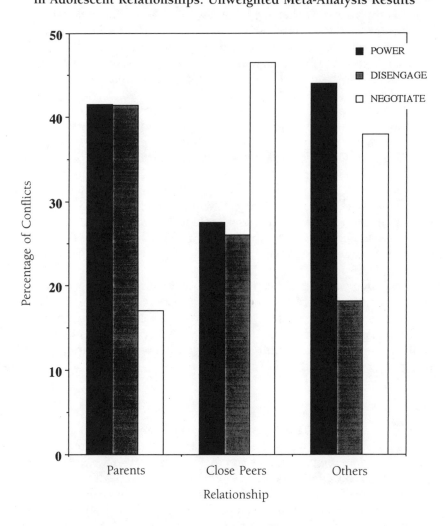

defined as disagreement: "You objected to something someone else said or did, or someone objected to what you said or did." Both measures encompassed several components of the conflict episode, including outcome. The telephone interview indicated the immediate outcome or end result of each conflict. The questionnaire assessed the conflict's impact on social interaction and its consequences for the relationship (see Laursen, 1993, for details).

The immediate outcome described the extent to which participants achieved their original goals: "What was the outcome of the disagreement? Did anyone get his or her way?" Two coders classified responses into one of three mutually exclusive categories: winner or loser, equitable, or no out-come. In the earlier example, Alice was clearly the winner and Ralph the loser. An equitable outcome entails a solution where both parties attain similar and roughly equal results. No outcome describes conflicts concluded without a solution, in which neither party attained his or her objectives. Interrater reliability for the coding of immediate outcomes was 90.1 percent (kappa = .86) on a subset of 350 randomly selected conflicts.

Postconflict social interaction described the disagreement's conse-quences for ongoing social interaction: "What happened immediately after the disagreement?" Adolescents selected one of three outcomes: stayed together and continued talking, stopped talking but stayed together, or no longer together. By remaining with Alice and pouting, Ralph discontinued verbal interaction but maintained physical proximity. This middle route can be contrasted with departure from the room to completely sever interaction and initiation of a new conversation to maintain social discourse.

The relationship impact described the perceived consequences of con-flict on relations between participants: "In what way did this disagreement affect your relationship?" Adolescents reported one of three outcomes: made the relationship better, no effect at all, or made the relationship worse. If all was quickly forgiven and forgotten between Alice and Ralph, then no relationship effects would be reported. It is conceivable, however, that the conflict proved especially enlightening to one of the participants, altering (for better or worse) behaviors toward and perceptions of the other.

Over half of the conflicts reported in the questionnaires and interviews involved parents (N's = 2,691 and 584, respectively); the rest were split between close peers (N's = 1,230 and 192, respectively) and other peers and adults (N's = 525 and 113, respectively). Separate analyses were conducted on each conflict outcome to explore differences within and across relation-ship categories. The following results describe significant multivariate anal-yses of variance and follow-up Tukey's honestly significant difference com-parisons (all p's < .01).

Immediate Outcomes: Telephone Interview Results. Close peer con-flicts were equally divided between winner or loser results and no outcome. In contrast, winner or loser outcomes predominated in disagreements with parents and others (see Figure 3.2). Across relationship categories, close peers reported fewer winner or loser outcomes and more no-outcome conflicts than reported with either parents or others. There were equally low levels of equitable outcomes across relationship categories.

Postconflict Social Interaction: Questionnaire Results. Within rela-tionship categories, most conflicts resulted in continued social interaction (see Figure 3.3). Across relationship categories, levels of continued social interaction were greatest among close peers; disputes with parents and others more often disrupted ongoing interactions.

Relationship Impact: Questionnaire Results. Within relationship cat-egories, most conflicts had no perceived impact on relations. Among close

Figure 3.2. Mean Proportion of Immediate Conflict Outcomes
in Adolescent Relationships: Telephone Interview Results

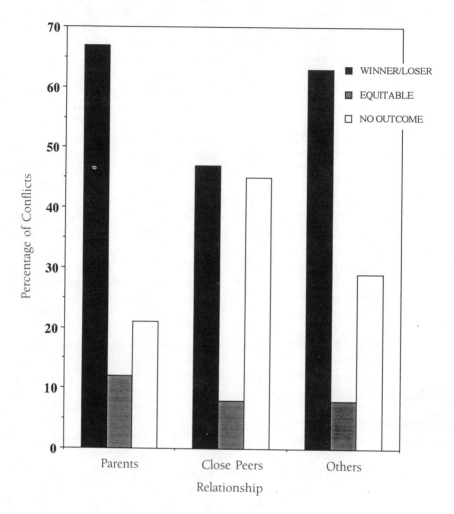

peers, conflict more often improved the relationship than made it worse. Parent-adolescent conflicts were equally likely to make the relationship better as worse. Among other peers and adults, conflict more often made the relationship worse than better (see Figure 3.4). Across relationship categories, conflict more often improved relations with close peers than with parents and others. Most of the conflicts that worsened relations arose with other peers and adults, whereas those with no relationship impact tended to involve parents.

Summary. In conflicts with close friends and romantic partners, adolescents avoided winner or loser outcomes, disrupted social interactions, and

Figure 3.3. Mean Proportion of Postconflict Social Interaction in
Adolescent Relationships: Questionnaire Results

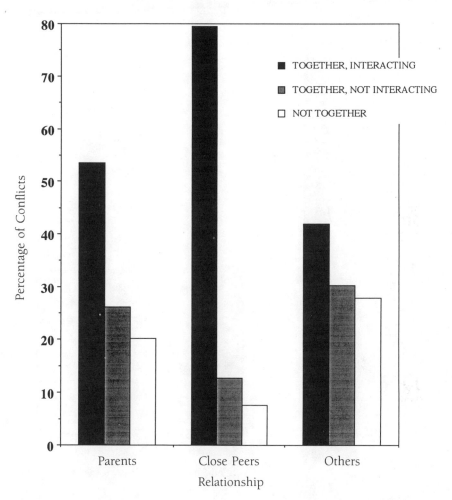

Source: Based on Laursen, 1993.

negative relationship effects. Compared to conflicts with close peers, disputes with parents and others more frequently entailed winner or loser outcomes and discontinued social interaction; although the parent-adolescent relationship was typically unaffected, almost one-third of all of the conflicts negatively affected relations with other peers and adults.

Process of Conflict Management

The following three examples selected from the telephone interviews highlight unique attributes of adolescent relationships. To illustrate process

**Figure 3.4. Mean Proportion of the Perceived Impact of
Conflict on Adolescent Relationships: Questionnaire Results**

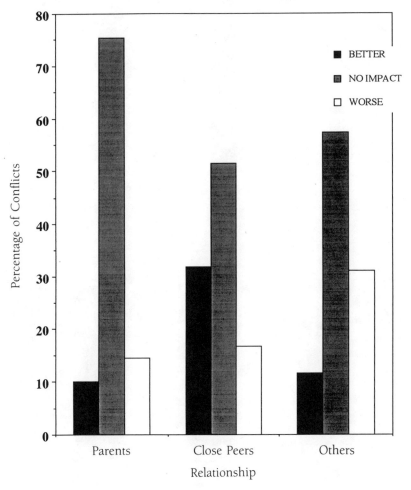

Source: Based on Laursen, 1993.

differences in conflict management, typical disputes with close peers, parents, and others, are compared.

Close Peers. Conflicts with close friends and romantic partners usually take place in private, over interpersonal issues. Frequently, they follow one of two paths. Some are resolved by disengagement, with no outcome and no impact on the relationship. Others are settled by negotiation, producing equitable outcomes and improving the relationship. In both cases, social interaction resumes afterward.

Ralph reported that this type of close peer conflict occurred while fishing with his best friend, Ed. Ralph really wanted to go to the junior prom with his girlfriend, Alice, but since she was grounded, he decided to take Alice's sister Trixie, instead. Ed thought that this decision was ill-advised and tried to convince Ralph not to invite Trixie. After some debate, the two hit on an alternative scheme: They would go to Alice's house and pretend to fight about taking Trixie to the prom, hoping the parents of the young women would be mortified enough to allow Alice to go after all. Having settled that problem, Ralph and Ed moved on to discuss their plans for prom night. Ralph reported that this conflict improved relations with his friend.

Parents. Adolescents' disagreements with parents typically begin with the adolescent alone at home, until a parent arrives and an argument ensues. According to adolescents, parents initiate disputes, typically over issues of autonomy, school, or responsibilities. Resolutions involve parental assertion of power, resulting in a winner (the parent) and a loser (the adolescent). The conflict concludes the interaction. Adolescents report that these conflicts are of little consequence to the relationship.

A few days prior to the disagreement with Ed described earlier, Alice was getting ready for school when her mother barged in and demanded to know why she was out so late the night before. Alice said that Ralph had had car troubles at a nearby lake and the repairs took a long time. Her mother was skeptical and an argument ensued. The discussion ended when Alice's mother grounded her for the remainder of the month and stalked out of the room. Even though Alice was now unable to attend the junior prom, she reportedly understood her mother's reaction and did not expect it to alter their relationship.

Other Relationships. Conflicts with employers, co-workers, teachers, and peers often begin in a public setting and concern issues of school or work. Most are resolved by power assertion, with winner or loser outcomes and discontinued social interaction. Conflicts are equally likely to affect the relationship negatively as have no impact.

In addition to his disagreement with Ed, Ralph also reported a conflict with his employer. Ralph had approached Mr. Mooney about getting out of work on prom night (despite the fact that he did not have a date). Over Ralph's objections, Mr. Mooney insisted that Ralph find a substitute worker for the evening. So Ralph lied and promised that Ed would work prom night. Without another word, he left Mr. Mooney's office. Ralph reported that this conflict made relations with his employer worse.

Relationship Features That Mitigate Close Peer Conflict Management

Why do close peers prefer negotiation and avoid power assertion? Three characteristics of adolescent relations with friends and romantic partners promote mitigating conflict resolution tactics: the voluntary nature of close peer relationships, the more-or-less even distribution of power and the reciprocity within them, and the issues and activities around which close peer interactions are organized.

Relationship Closeness. According to equity theory (Kelley and others, 1983), individuals with personal histories of rewarding social exchanges strive to maintain relationships (and rewards) by reducing distress and inequity. The longer the duration that two parties have been in a close relationship, the more each is invested in continuing it. When inequity develops, the challenge is to correct the imbalance without jeopardizing ongoing interactions. Relationships with close friends and romantic partners are somewhat tenuous and easily disrupted; close peer relationships can be, and often are, severed over a single dispute—a situation that adolescents readily recognize and anticipate (Hartup, 1992; Selman, 1980). The maintenance of a close association during difficult times is a delicate task requiring negotiation.

Adolescents are not heavily invested in relationships with teachers, employers, peers, and co-workers, nor are they overly concerned with maintaining interactions that are not rewarding. As a consequence, conflict resolution tactics are focused on winning the dispute, unconstrained by relationship considerations. Power assertion is common, even though it frequently worsens the relationship. Provocation of the boss could cost Ralph his job, but aside from this unlikely consequence there are few relationship sanctions to discourage escalation of the conflict and an inequitable outcome.

Family members are also less concerned than are close peers about the long-term impact of conflict on the relationship, although for different reasons. Family ties represent closed relationships, defined by kinship, norms, and laws (Berscheid, 1985; Collins and Laursen, 1992). Families are stable, as close to permanent as adolescent relationships typically become. Members of the relationship, therefore, are freer to exhibit conflict behaviors that might disrupt less permanent bonds. Thus, no matter the resolution or outcome of the curfew dispute, Alice will still eat breakfast with her parents and probably even ask to borrow the family car. Life with mother inevitably returns to normal.

In contrast, open relationships with close peers are competitive and unstable (Berscheid, 1985; Collins and Laursen, 1992). To maintain rewarding exchanges, adolescents must be sensitive to the possibility that a short-term conflict victory achieved at any cost may result in long-term disruption of the relationship. Since close peer relationships are initiated and dissolved with some frequency, Ralph must always be aware that Ed has other options for friends should their relationship go awry.

Relationship Reciprocity. A second attribute of close peer relationships that favors negotiated conflicts and equitable outcomes is the mutual and reciprocal nature of these affiliations. Children and adolescents maintain relationships in two different social worlds: one with peers, who must share power, and one with adults, who expect submission (Hartup, 1979; Piaget, [1932] 1965). An uneven distribution of power invites one side to take advantage of the other, whereas a level playing field promotes negotiation and equity in outcome.

Peer relationships are horizontal in that both parties hold roughly equal power. In order for peers to get along, agreement and cooperation must prevail. When confronted with an opponent of equal and known power, cooperation is the most productive and least risky resolution strategy (Deutsch, 1973). By avoiding power assertion, the adolescents avert mutually assured destruction. Therefore, given the option, negotiation and bargaining are preferred modes of resolving differences between close friends and romantic partners (Cowan, Drinkard, and MacGavin, 1984; Youniss and Smollar, 1985). Ed knows that his attempt to force a resolution on Ralph may backfire; the conflict may escalate and Ralph may ultimately prevail. Better to settle for a mutually satisfactory resolution than risk losing altogether.

Adult-child relationships are different. In these vertical associations, one party typically dominates the other. Adolescents describe relationships with parents and other adults as unilateral, characterized by an imbalance of power (Furman and Buhrmester, 1985; Youniss and Smollar, 1985). Power assertion is common in adult-adolescent disagreements, as adults impose their will on those with lesser status (Barker and Wright, 1955; Smetana, Yau, and Hanson, 1991). Thus, Alice's mother and Ralph's boss were able to dictate the terms of conflict resolution, leaving neither adolescent with any recourse but submission.

Relationship Issues and Activities. The third attribute of close peer relationships that promotes equitable resolutions concerns the issues and activities central to adolescent interactions, which can be sources of disagreement and conflict. Distinct conflict issues arise with parents and peers that are directly related to the experiences that they share (see Collins and Laursen, 1992, for review). Conflicts with close peers frequently concern interpersonal trust and behavior, whereas conflicts with parents typically involve rules, school, and chores. Simply put, close friends and romantic partners disagree over issues that are more readily negotiated than those arising in other relationships.

Interactions with close peers consist mainly of free time spent in leisure activities (Laursen, 1989). Typically, conflict centers on long-standing, ongoing interpersonal concerns, comprising a tangled skein of interchanges carried forward across time and settings (Goodwin and Goodwin, 1987). Misunderstandings of words or deeds are not uncommon and are compounded by the misreporting ("he said, she said") of helpful peers. Simple solutions to these complex issues are elusive. Hence negotiation ("talking things out") is the preferred method of resolving the important issues of friendship and romance. Solutions to personal problems cannot be dictated or imposed, so power assertion is uncommon (Selman and others, 1986; Youniss and Smollar, 1985). Although Ralph's initial scheme was clearly muddled, Ed worked with him to achieve a satisfactory solution to the problem, rather than simply insist that he not take Trixie to the prom.

Relationships with parents and other adults take place primarily during task time filled with chores, schoolwork, and other nonleisure activities

(Laursen, 1989). The settings involve clearly defined standards of behavior for participants. Parent-adolescent conflict issues are non-negotiable. When parental expectations are violated, sanctions must be imposed. Discipline, by definition, encompasses power assertion. Parents resolve these conflicts by issuing directives and commands, to which adolescents have little choice but to submit (Smetana, Yau, and Hanson, 1991; Youniss and Smollar, 1985). Consequently, when Alice missed curfew, she was in no position to bargain because her mother always prevails in these disputes.

Conclusion

Although all experiences overlap somewhat, the nature and function of adolescent relations with close friends and romantic partners provide a context for social development quite distinct from that with parents and others. Close peers shape and control the acquisition of many essential social skills, including the ability to resolve interpersonal conflict (Hartup and Laursen, 1991). In no other type of relationship does the child learn the delicate art of negotiation and conciliation. During the adolescent years, abilities further develop to keep pace with increasingly sophisticated peer relationships (Hartup, 1992).

Conflicts with close peers tend to be resolved through compromise, which provides mutually satisfactory solutions, continued social interactions, and even improved relations. Three features of close peer relationships contribute to this pattern of conflict management. First, voluntary relationships are vulnerable to disruption, and one poorly managed dispute can threaten a major interpersonal investment. Second, horizontal or egalitarian relationships require consensus and agreement. Negotiation is the most pragmatic way to settle disagreements between those of equal power. Finally, close peer interactions are organized around leisure activities, where cooperation is of paramount concern.

Close peers provide a context for the development of negotiation skills. Indeed, they demand it. No other kind of adolescent relationship is constrained by attributes that oblige participants to resolve differences in a manner that keeps everyone happy. What differentiates the conflict management patterns of adolescent friends and romantic partners from those of other kinds of relationships? The structure of the relationship requires compromise for the affiliation to survive and thrive.

Appendix: Studies Used in the Meta-Analysis

Hobart, C. J. "Preadolescents' and Adolescents' Conflicts with Siblings and Friends." Paper presented at the biennial meeting of the Society for Research in Child Development, Seattle, Apr. 1991.

Laursen, B. "Relationships and Conflict During Adolescence." Unpublished doctoral dissertation, Institute of Child Development, University of Minnesota, 1989.

Leyva, F. A., and Furth, H. G. "Compromise Formation in Social Conflicts: The Influence of Age, Issue, and Interpersonal Context." *Journal of Youth and Adolescence,* 1986, *15,* 441–452.

Montemayor, R., and Hanson, E. "A Naturalistic View of Conflict Between Adolescents and Their Parents and Siblings." *Journal of Early Adolescence,* 1985, *5,* 23–30.

Raffaelli, M. "Sibling Conflict in Early Adolescence." Unpublished doctoral dissertation, Committee on Human Development, University of Chicago, 1990.

Richardson, D. R., Hammock, G. S., Lubben, T., and Mickler, S. "The Relationship Between Love Attitudes and Conflict Responses." *Journal of Social and Clinical Psychology,* 1989, *8,* 430–441.

Sillars, A. L. "Attributions and Communication in Roommate Conflicts." *Communication Monographs,* 1980, *47,* 180–200.

Smetana, J. G., Yau, J., and Hanson, S. "Conflict Resolution in Families with Adolescents." *Journal of Research on Adolescence,* 1991, *1,* 189–206.

Teismann, M. W., and Mosher, D. L. "Jealous Conflict in Dating Couples." *Psychological Reports,* 1978, *42,* 1211–1216.

Utley, M. E., Richardson, D. R., and Pilkington, C. J. "Personality and Interpersonal Conflict Management." *Personality and Individual Differences,* 1989, *10,* 287–293.

Vuchinich, S. "Starting and Stopping Spontaneous Family Conflicts." *Journal of Marriage and the Family,* 1987, *49,* 591–601.

Youniss, J., and Smollar, J. *Adolescent Relations with Mothers, Fathers, and Friends.* Chicago: University of Chicago Press, 1985.

References

Barker, R. G., and Wright, H. F. *Midwest and Its Children.* New York: HarperCollins, 1955.

Berscheid, E. "Interpersonal Attraction." In G. Lindzey and E. Aronson (eds.), *Handbook of Social Psychology.* New York: Random House, 1985.

Cohen, J. *Statistical Power Analysis for the Behavioral Sciences.* (Rev. ed.) San Diego: Academic Press, 1977.

Collins, W. A., and Laursen, B. "Conflict and Relationships During Adolescence." In C. U. Shantz and W. W. Hartup (eds.), *Conflict in Child and Adolescent Development.* New York: Cambridge University Press, 1992.

Cowan, G., Drinkard, J., and MacGavin, L. "The Effects of Target, Age, and Gender on Use of Power Strategies." *Journal of Personality and Social Psychology,* 1984, *47,* 1391–1398.

Deutsch, M. *The Resolution of Conflict.* New Haven, Conn.: Yale University Press, 1973.

Furman, W., and Buhrmester, D. "Children's Perceptions of the Personal Relationships in Their Social Networks." *Developmental Psychology,* 1985, *21,* 1016–1024.

Goodwin, M. H., and Goodwin, C. "Children's Arguing." In S. Phillips, S. Steele, and C. Tanz (eds.), *Language, Gender, and Sex in Comparative Perspective.* New York: Cambridge University Press, 1987.

Hartup, W. W. "The Social Worlds of Childhood." *American Psychologist,* 1979, *34,* 944–950.

Hartup, W. W. "Conflict and Friendship Relations." In C. U. Shantz and W. W. Hartup (eds.), *Conflict in Child and Adolescent Development.* New York: Cambridge University Press, 1992.

Hartup, W. W., and Laursen, B. "Relationships as Developmental Contexts." In R. Cohen and A. W. Siegel (eds.), *Context and Development.* Hillsdale, N.J.: Erlbaum, 1991.

Hartup, W. W., and Laursen, B. "Conflict and Context in Peer Relations." In C. Hart (ed.), *Children on Playgrounds: Research Perspectives and Applications.* Albany: State University of New York Press, 1993.

Hedges, L., and Olkin, I. *Statistical Methods for Meta-Analysis.* San Diego: Academic Press, 1985.

Kelley, H. H., Berscheid, E., Christensen, A., Harvey, J. H., Huston, T. L., Levinger, G., McClintock, E., Peplau, L. A., and Peterson, D. E. *Close Relationships.* New York: Freeman, 1983.

Laursen, B. "Relationships and Conflict During Adolescence." Unpublished doctoral thesis, Institute of Child Development, University of Minnesota, 1989.

Laursen, B. "The Perceived Impact of Conflict on Adolescent Relationships." *Merrill-Palmer Quarterly,* 1993, *39,* 535–550.

Perry, D. G., Perry, L. C., and Kennedy, E. "Conflict and the Development of Antisocial Behavior." In C. U. Shantz and W. W. Hartup (eds.), *Conflict in Child and Adolescent Development.* New York: Cambridge University Press, 1992.

Piaget, J. *The Moral Judgment of the Child.* New York: Free Press, 1965. (Originally published 1932.)

Prinz, R. J., Foster, S. L., Kent, R. N., and O'Leary, K. D. "Multivariate Assessment of Conflict in Distressed and Non-Distressed Mother-Adolescent Dyads." *Journal of Applied Behavior Analysis,* 1979, *12,* 691–700.

Robin, A. L., and Foster, S. L. "Problem-Solving Communication Training: A Behavioral Family Systems Approach to Parent-Adolescent Conflict." In P. Karoly and J. J. Steffen (eds.), *Adolescent Behavior Disorders: Foundations and Contemporary Concerns.* Lexington, Mass.: Heath, 1984.

Selman, R. L. *The Growth of Interpersonal Understanding: Developmental and Clinical Analyses.* San Diego: Academic Press, 1980.

Selman, R. L., Beardslee, W., Schultz, L. H., Krupa, M., and Poderefsky, D. "Assessing Adolescent Interpersonal Negotiation Strategies: Toward the Integration of Structural and Functional Models." *Developmental Psychology,* 1986, *22,* 450–459.

Shantz, C. U. "Conflict Between Children." *Child Development,* 1987, *58,* 283–305.

Shantz, C. U., and Hobart, C. J. "Social Conflict and Development: Peers and Siblings." In T. J. Berndt and G. W. Ladd (eds.), *Peer Relationships in Child Development.* New York: Wiley, 1989.

Smetana, J. G., Yau, J., and Hanson, S. "Conflict Resolution in Families with Adolescents." *Journal of Research on Adolescence,* 1991, *1,* 189–206.

Vuchinich, S. "The Sequential Organization of Closing in Verbal Family Conflict." In A. D. Grimshaw (ed.), *Conflict Talk: Sociolinguistic Investigations of Arguments in Conversations.* New York: Cambridge University Press, 1990.

Youniss, J., and Smollar, J. *Adolescent Relations with Mothers, Fathers, and Friends.* Chicago: University of Chicago Press, 1985.

BRETT LAURSEN is assistant professor of psychology at Florida Atlantic University.

Based on family systems theory, a typology of close friendships in adolescence is presented. Close friends' ability to negotiate closeness and separateness is different in early and middle adolescence. These differences are also reflected in partners' levels of friendship reasoning.

Close Friendships in Early and Middle Adolescence: Typology and Friendship Reasoning

Shmuel Shulman

Friendships can be found throughout the life span. For young children, friends are partners or playmates with whom time is spent and interesting activities can be pursued (Ginsberg, Gottman, and Parker, 1986; Howes, 1981). With age, though common activities continue to reflect an important aspect of friendship, friends are also willing to help one another (Wright, 1984) and feel a special obligation to be responsive to one another's needs. The degree to which two friends share and help each other indicates the closeness of their relationship (Berndt, 1986).

With the emergence of the need for intimate relationships in adolescence (Sullivan, 1953), friends become open to one another, disclose personal secrets, and exchange ideas within a secure and accepting environment. Studies have found that adolescents emphasize self-disclosure, openness, and affection as crucial components of their friendships (Berndt, 1986; Bigelow, 1977; Furman and Bierman, 1983; Hunter and Youniss, 1982). Sharing of intimate feelings is the hallmark of close friendship and distinguishes it from "common" friendship (Oden, Hertzberger, Mangaine, and Wheeler, 1984).

Most previous studies of friendship and its functions have been based on interviews with children regarding their friendships and their conceptions of friendship (Bigelow, 1977; Ginsberg, Gottman, and Parker, 1986; Youniss, 1980). In the study described here, a different approach to adolescents' close friendships—a systems perspective—is presented. Relationships and friendships are viewed not as individual features but rather as dyadic, systematic processes (Hartup, 1986; Hinde, 1979). A system is a set of units or elements that bear a consistent relationship or interactional stance to one another. In addition, processes in a system are governed by general principles (Bertalanffy, 1968). Relationships within the system reflect coordination among elements where inclinations are negotiated with an emphasis on wholeness.

A Systems Approach to Friendship: Theoretical Background

Research on friendship dyads has documented that friends interact differently from nonfriends when working on a task (Charlesworth and LaFreniere, 1983; Newcomb and Brady, 1982). Friends are attentive to each other, and interaction is harmonious and aimed at an equal distribution of rewards. However, real-world circumstances do not always allow equal distribution of rewards among friends; there are conditions where winners take everything. Hartup (1983) has reported that in winner-take-all conditions, hostility and self-interest prevail. But these are not the only conditions that arouse competition between individuals and friends. The need to express self-interest and individualism also plays a role in friendships. Along with the growing need for intimate close friends during adolescence (Sullivan, 1953; Youniss, 1980), there is a growing need for self-expression and individuality (Blos, [1967] 1979).

Individual interests or inclinations may lead to disagreements and conflicts, even in well-functioning relationships (Hartup, Laursen, Stewart, and Eastenson, 1988). Yet friends resolve their conflicts in a manner that does not adversely affect their relationship. Friends are less tense in conflicts; they negotiate or disengage and show less tendency to stand firm. Friends are capable of working out the dialectics of common interests that emphasize cooperation and agreement, on the one hand, and individual needs, which may be opposing and lead to competition and disagreement, on the other.

A number of questions are raised by these observations. Are all disagreements between friends resolved in a similar manner? Are there dyads who optimally balance cooperation and individuality? Are there some dyads who emphasize cooperation and suppress individual needs, and other dyads who insist more on individual needs and disengage from conflict? These questions clearly delineate "systemic" dilemmas concerning how elements or units in a system coordinate relationships among themselves within the framework of the general system. Systems theory has been successfully applied in the field of family relationships (Steinglass, 1978), and the application of the systems approach to close friendships may bring similar advances.

The problem of balancing closeness and individuality in close relationships is central to the field of family systems. Wynne (1958, 1970) was among the first to conceptualize and describe the nature of family relations. According to Wynne, there is a basic need for affection and warmth in human contact. In addition, individuals in the family strive for self-differentiation and achievement of their own goals. Other theorists have conceptualized two similar dimensions in the family system: emotional relatedness among family members and the striving of each family member for personal development and independence (Minuchin, 1974; Olson, Sprenkle, and Russel, 1979). Reiss (1981) formulated a theory on the varieties of family consensual experience that describes the nature of members' closeness. Utilizing a joint problem-solving task, he derived three main dimensions of family interaction: (1) *configuration,* or problem-solving effectiveness, which refers to the contribution of the family in enhancing individual problem solving when the entire family works as a group; (2) *coordination,* which refers to the will, determination, and capacity of family members to solve problems in a similar manner; and (3) *closure,* which reflects whether family members quickly agree on their approach or more slowly reach their decision following an evaluation of all information. Based on the interplay between efficient individual problem solving and family coordination, Reiss suggested three main family types:

Environment-sensitive paradigm. When a problem is presented to the family, each member is aware of the need to use and explore the available stimuli and information in order to solve the problem. As a group aiming to achieve the best possible solution, they objectively react to one another and are free to accept or reject one another's solutions. There is no pressure to accept the particular solution offered by any member. The information presented by each member is helpful in clarifying the problem and reaching the optimal solution. The final solution is a balance between individual perceptions and group contributions. In this paradigm, individual and family needs are truly balanced.

Consensus-sensitive paradigm. In families of this type, it is most important for members to be cohesive and in full agreement with one another. Each member is sensitive to the opinions of the others and does not express ideas that may clash with or hurt another member. In an effort to remain united and work cooperatively, the family strives to reach a quick solution to the problem without disagreements. This overemphasis on cohesion prevents them from examining all of the facts, so the solution reached is not always the most effective. Individuality and its expression (competition) are suppressed in favor of a sense of closeness.

Distance-sensitive paradigm. Problem solving in this type of family is perceived as a way for each member to express independence from the others. The acceptance of another's opinion is evidence of weakness. Each member attempts to solve the problem without using any information provided by other family members. Some members work quickly and impulsively, while others methodically examine all of the data. In this paradigm, family members barely cooperate, seeking instead to demonstrate control over and independence from one another.

Reiss's family typology is conceptually similar to other family typologies (Olson, Sprenkle, and Russel, 1979; Wynne, 1958). The merit of his approach is that it is experimentally based, whereas others are based on clinical experience with families. Furthermore, his approach highlights possible solutions to the problem of balancing closeness and cooperation as well as individuality and competition in close relationships.

Application of these family paradigms within the arena of adolescent close friendships suggests three types of relationships. In the first, friends are close to each other; intimacy and self-disclosure mark this type of friendship. However, closeness is not achieved at the expense of either partner's independence. This type parallels Reiss's environment-sensitive paradigm and reflects interdependence between close friends. In the second type of friendship, intimacy and closeness between partners are overemphasized, even at the expense of individuality. This type parallels the consensus-sensitive paradigm. Sometimes the emphasis on intimacy leads to a possessive relationship, where partners insist on each other's availability and responsibility in all circumstances (Berndt, 1983). In the third type of friendship, partners overemphasize individuality, which parallels the distance-sensitive paradigm. Although it may not seem logical to propose a close friendship type in which partners prefer separateness, the behavior is consistent with that of middle-childhood friends who are unable to cooperate when facing a task that arouses competition (Berndt, 1987).

Recent studies of social cognition have also contributed to our understanding of friendship in children and adolescents (Berndt, 1983; Gottman and Mettetal, 1986; Selman, 1980). At early stages, friends are perceived as playmates and later as cooperative partners. Only in middle childhood and adolescence do children start to deal with issues of intimacy and closeness. Selman (1980) has proposed an elaborate model of friendship development, with two sequential stages in adolescence. At the initial stage, close friendship is characterized by mutual support and understanding; at the later stage, friends are able to balance intimacy and closeness with respect for individuality.

Selman (1988) has suggested four different levels of shared experience among children. At level 0, the lowest, experience is shared when one child imitates the other. At level 1, children, through expressive enthusiasm, take turns imitating each other in a more conscious way and continually share their experiences. At level 2, shared experience is based on reciprocal reflection. Each partner reflects on his or her own experience for the sake of self-satisfaction, without a strong sense of interconnecting experiences. What is important at this level is the closeness and the sense that somebody is listening. At level 3, the highest, there is greater concern for one's partner and a capability of incorporating the other's experience into an integrated "we." According to Selman, the major difference between the two highest levels is cooperation for self-interest (level 2) versus collaboration for mutual interest (level 3).

Taken together, Selman's friendship reasoning levels describe different balances within the friendship system. For example, there are friendships aimed at self-interest, and friendships marked by mutual interest. The question is whether members of a friendship system who optimally balance closeness and individuality exhibit higher levels of friendship reasoning than achieved by members of a friendship system who are either too close or too distant.

A systems approach suggests that in an optimal close friendship in adolescence the partners are able to balance closeness and intimacy with individuality. However, it is not clear that the ability to achieve this optimal balance exists across the different stages of adolescence. Thus, close friendships in early and middle adolescence must be investigated to determine whether developmental stages affect the types of close friendship systems that adolescents establish. Within this general framework of inquiry, the present study had three objectives. The first was to apply the systems approach to close friendships in adolescence in order to examine whether there are different types of friendships, paralleling Reiss's (1981) earlier described typology of families. The second objective was to examine whether there are differences between early and middle adolescence in friendship types. The third objective was to examine adolescents' conceptions of friendship across the range of friendship types. Pursuit of the final two objectives was, of course, contingent on the results of the first objective.

Method

Subjects. The study sample was drawn from 147 seventh graders (median age = 12 years, age range = 11.4–13.1) and 161 tenth graders (median age = 15 years, age range = 14.6–15.9) from a junior and a senior high school in two suburbs of Tel Aviv, Israel. The students represented a wide spectrum of social classes. Homeroom teachers were asked to identify pairs of same-sex close friends in their classes. Subsequently, popular and socially active students were also asked to identify pairs of close friends. Finally, identified subjects were individually interviewed about their close friends. Pairs rated how well they liked their close friends on a 7-point scale. Only those pairs identified by teachers and friends as reciprocal close friendships were included in the study. More than 90 percent of the subjects rated their close friends at the highest level of liking. From this procedure, 41 pairs of early adolescent close friends (24 pairs of girls and 17 pairs of boys) and 45 pairs of middle adolescent close friends (23 pairs of girls and 22 pairs of boys) were included in the study.

Classification of Friendships and Friendship Reasoning. In order to examine the issue of types of friendship systems, pairs of close friends were given the Reiss card-sort procedure, and subjects were individually interviewed concerning their joint daily activities. In addition, the Selman (1980) Friendship Conceptions Interview was individually administered to examine friendship reasoning. In half of the cases, the joint card-sort task was administered before the individuals were interviewed. In the other half, the order was reversed.

Reiss Card-Sort Procedure. A problem-solving procedure, detailed in Reiss (1981), was given to both friends. It consists of a set of cards that each show a row of letters, varying in order and length within the set. Subjects are asked to sort the cards in any way they choose and into as many piles as they choose, up to seven. Cards may be sorted according to pattern or length. The task is divided into two phases. First, friends sort the cards individually, without speaking to each other. Second, friends are permitted to talk to and to consult with each other while sorting the cards, but they are not instructed about whether or not they must reach an agreement. Two cards are sorted at a time, and the tester permits them to go on to the next two cards after both are finished. The possible patterns for each of the two phases are similar in form, but not identical.

The dimensions postulated by Reiss as characterizing types of family interaction are represented by measures of behavior, produced by objective recording during the procedure. The configuration dimension is represented by two measures that indicate the pair's problem-solving effectiveness: the Individual Sort and the Joint Sort. The coordination dimension is represented by the interfriend Sort Similarity measure and the standard deviation of members' trial-ending times, Time SD. A low Time SD reflects friends' tendency to finish each trial together. Changes in the configuration scores from the initial to the joint phase reflect the extent to which friends influence each other when interaction and consultation are permitted. A stable configuration score or a positive change implies that interaction between friends does not harm and even improves their problem-solving performance. A negative change implies that interaction between friends leads to a deterioration in problem-solving ability. A high coordination score (high Sort Similarity and low Time SD) indicates that friends work as a coordinated pair. A low coordination score (low Sort Similarity and high Time SD) implies that individual styles of card sorting resist reciprocal influence. Classification of pairs into relationship types is based on configuration and coordination scores (see Reiss, 1981). The classification of friendship pairs in the present study is detailed in the Results section.

Daily Activities Interview. To better understand the nature of possible friendship types, subjects were asked to describe common activities with close friends, including type, frequency, and location of their meetings and activities. They were also asked to describe how often they met as dyads and in groups. Closeness was verified by interview questions such as whether they slept at each other's homes, swapped clothing, and touched each other in playful activities. Two raters coded adolescents' responses; interrater agreement ranged between 91 and 100 percent across friendship activities.

Friendship Conceptions Interview. Subjects were given Selman's (1980) hypothetical friendship dilemma. A written dilemma was presented and subjects were instructed to write down their opinions in detail. The friendship issues explored were (1) motivation ("Friendship is important to me because . . . "), (2) jealousy ("If Dan is jealous of Gad because of his interaction with Eitan, it will cause their friendship to . . . "), (3) conflict ("Sometimes conflicts occur between friends because . . . "), and (4) termination of friendship ("A close friendship terminates when . . . "). Answers were scored by two raters according to the procedures prescribed by Selman and Jaquette (1977); interrater agreement on issues ranged between 86 and 91 percent. For each subject, the ratings yielded an individual score on a 0–3 rating scale, paralleling Selman's (1988) friendship reasoning stages; agreement between the two raters was 89 percent.

Adolescents' responses on the four friendship issues also were content-analyzed following Youniss's (1980) approach. First, four reasons were given by subjects as motivation for establishing friendships: avoid loneliness, joint activities, help and support, and intimacy and disclosure. Second, jealousy was perceived as leading to either separation between friends or change and development in the relationship. Third, two reasons were given to explain conflicts between friends: differing ideas and mistrust or jealousy within the relationship. Finally, three reasons for termination of a friendship were mentioned: fighting, mistrust and jealousy, and change or development of one partner or growing interest in the opposite sex. Subjects' responses on the four friendship issues were scored in terms of whether they mentioned or did not mention each reason. Agreement between the two raters ranged from 86 to 91 percent.

Cooperation and Noncooperation Reasoning. Early adolescent subjects were individually asked why they had cooperated (or not cooperated) on the card sort. In addition, they were asked to reflect on the reasoning of those who acted differently from them. Content analysis yielded two distinct reasons for cooperation and two for noncooperation. The reasons for cooperation were "It is fun to work together; we are friends" and "You cooperate when you need help." The reasons for noncooperation were "preference for working individually" and "conflict."

Results

Results for early and for middle adolescents are separately presented here. First, the classification and characterization of friendship types are described. Second, the levels of friendship reasoning across friendship types in both age cohorts are presented.

Classification of Close Friendships in Early Adolescence. Performance on the Reiss card-sort procedure indicated two main types of friendships: interdependent and disengaged. The majority, twenty-eight pairs, hardly interacted during the joint problem-solving task, even though they had been encouraged to consult each other. As presented in Table 4.1, their Sort Similarity score was low and their Time SD was high. These two measures indicate that friends worked individually and completed their tasks at different paces. In addition, the level of joint task complexity was lower than that in the initial individual stage, suggesting that interaction produced less effective problem solving. These disengaged pairs resembled Reiss's distance-sensitive family type. In contrast, the thirteen interdependent pairs were high on coordination; their sets were high on Sort Similarity, and joint work did not have a negative impact on their level of configuration. These pairs resembled the environment-sensitive family type. In sum, two main types of close friendships were found. The first, disengaged friends, consisted of pairs who considered themselves close friends, but when given a joint task, they were not coordinated and tended to work individually. The second, interdependent friends, consisted of pairs who cooperated and coordinated their activities.

Classification of Close Friendships in Middle Adolescence. In this age group as well, the same two close friendship types emerged, but the patterns were reversed. Thirty-six of the forty-five pairs revealed high levels of configuration and coordination. As presented in Table 4.1, there was no significant change in problem-solving effectiveness from initial to joint trials; the levels of problem solving remained high. Joint solutions were similar, and the pairs tended to complete the task simultaneously. These interdependent dyads resembled Reiss's environment-sensitive family type. In contrast, the nine disengaged pairs were high on configuration and low on coordination. Although their level of configuration was similar to that of the interdependent pairs, they clearly differed on level of coordination. These friends

Table 4.1. Card-Sort Measures Across the Two
Friendship Types: Early and Middle Adolescence

	Early Adolescence		Middle Adolescence	
	Interdependent (N = 13)	*Disengaged* (N = 28)	*Interdependent* (N = 36)	*Disengaged* (N = 9)
Configuration				
Initial complexity	0.76	0.82	0.84	0.80
Joint complexity	0.76	0.70	0.84	0.83
Coordination				
Sort similarity	0.94	0.53	0.98	0.55
Time SD	3.71	17.51	1.54	5.59

Note: N = number of dyads.

worked individually on the joint task, solved the problem differently, and tended to complete the task at their own pace. These pairs resembled the distance-sensitive family type.

Summary. Male and female subjects were equally distributed across friendship types in both age cohorts. Only two close friendship types emerged: interdependent and disengaged. In early adolescence, 61 percent of close friends did not cooperate when given a joint task, whereas in middle adolescence, 80 percent of close friends cooperated on the joint task ($\chi^2 = 18.64$, df = 1, $p < .001$).

Daily Activities Across Friendship Types. Interviews revealed similar activities across friendship types in both age cohorts. Friends met four or five times per week after school and spoke on the telephone at least once a day. They met at one of the friends' homes or somewhere outside the home. They went to the beach, to movies, or to parties together. They also studied together. Sleeping over at the friend's home was not common, but they frequently exchanged educational material, items of clothing, and records. There were no significant differences in the nature, location, and frequency of joint activities across the two friendship types in either age group. Disengaged pairs participated in activities similar to those of interdependent pairs. The only difference was that disengaged pairs were less likely than interdependent pairs to go out together, preferring instead to visit each other at home. Thus, although interdependent and disengaged pairs behaved differently on the joint task, they were similar in the nature of their daily activities and interests.

Friendship Reasoning and Friendship Types in Early Adolescence. Written answers on the Friendship Conceptions Interview indicated that the friendship reasoning level of friends who cooperated on the joint task ($M = 1.61$, SD = 0.39) was similar to that of friends who did not cooperate ($M = 1.50$, SD = 0.48). These levels of friendship reasoning correspond to levels reported for twelve-year-olds in other non-U.S. samples (Keller and Wood, 1989). Reasoning responses on friendship issues also did not indicate differences between interdependent and disengaged pairs.

Early adolescents were also asked to reflect on reasons for cooperation or noncooperation with their close friends. Early adolescent interdependent friends gave different reasons for cooperation and noncooperation from those of disengaged friends.

As indicated in Table 4.2, interdependent friends perceived consultation and cooperation as basic to their relationships. They reported that it was fun or great to work together. Disengaged dyads approved of cooperation when necessary, but not for the sake of friendship. Regarding reasons for noncooperation, disengaged pairs clearly preferred to work individually; they saw no need for cooperation when the task was easy and manageable. Interdependent friends accepted noncooperation only in cases where cooperation was attempted but failed.

Table 4.2. Reasons for Cooperation and Noncooperation in
Interdependent and Disengaged Early Adolescent Friendships

Reasons	Interdependent	Disengaged
Cooperation[a]		
Enjoy working together	21	9
Need help	13	20
Noncooperation[b]		
Prefer to work individually	7	27
Unable to cooperate (in conflict)	19	8

Note: Figures represent numbers of subjects.

[a] $\chi^2 = 6.91$, df = 1, $p < .01$.

[b] $\chi^2 = 15.26$, df = 1, $p < .001$.

Friendship Reasoning and Friendship Types in Middle Adolescence.
Comparison of friendship types in this age group revealed a significant
difference in the level of friendship reasoning between interdependent
friends ($M = 2.17$, $SD = 0.68$) and disengaged friends ($M = 1.39$,
$SD = 0.69$; $t = 3.06$, $p < .01$). Middle adolescents' reasoning responses on
the friendship issues were also content-analyzed and the distribution of the
various categories across the two friendship types was tallied. As indicated
in Table 4.3, the interdependent and the disengaged friends reported
different reasons for friendship.

Disengaged pairs looked for close friends out of fear of loneliness, but
they were less inclined than interdependent pairs to view friendship as an
arena for joint activities for support. Thus, adolescents in disengaged pairs
had different motivations for having a close friend from those of adolescents
in interdependent pairs. Intimacy, however, was a common theme in both
types of friendship.

Jealousy was generally seen to lead to either separation or to change in
the course of the friendship. Disengaged adolescents tended to perceive
jealousy as a reason for separation. Differences of opinion were also sources
of conflict between friends in the disengaged pairs. Interdependent friends,
on the other hand, typically emphasized matters of trust and jealousy as
sources of conflict.

Three reasons for the termination of a friendship were raised by adolescents across friendship types: a conflict between friends, mistrust, and
personal changes, for instance, the intrusion of a third person (a boyfriend
or girlfriend). Interdependent pairs emphasized mistrust, jealousy, and
change; disengaged adolescents typically emphasized fights. Thus, while
adolescents in the disengaged pairs mainly looked for close friends to assuage
loneliness, their sense of closeness was not strong. For them, differences of
opinion could lead to conflict, and conflict to friendship termination.
Adolescents in the interdependent pairs had a more solid view of friendship,
and conflicts were not perceived as threats to their relationships.

Table 4.3. Reasoning on Four Friendship Issues Across Two Types of Close Friendships in Middle Adolescence

Friendship Issues	Interdependent (N = 72)	Disengaged (N = 18)	χ^2
Friendship is important for what?			
Not being lonely	11 (18)	12 (5)	15.43
Joint activities	14 (12)	2 (4)	(df = 3, $p < .01$)
Help, support	32 (29)	4 (8)	
Intimacy	37 (36)	10 (11)	
What can jealousy do to a friendship?			
Separation	23 (26)	8 (5)	3.26
Change, development	56 (54)	7 (10)	(df = 1, $p < .09$)
What are the reasons for a conflict between friends?			
Different opinions, ideas	22 (26)	10 (6)	4.54
Misunderstanding, change in trust, jealousy	49 (45)	7 (11)	(df = 1, $p < .04$)
What may end a friendship?			
Conflict	17 (21)	8 (4)	7.36
Mistrust, jealousy	39 (40)	7 (8)	(df = 2, $p < .03$)
Change, development, third person	31 (27)	2 (5)	

Note: Figures are numbers of subjects; parenthetical figures are expected frequencies, rounded.

Summary. The two types of close friendship differed in friendship reasoning. Middle adolescents raised different reasons for having a friend and emphasized different reasons for terminating a friendship. Differences in early adolescent friendship reasoning were revealed.

Discussion

Age-related differences emerged in types of friendship and reasoning about friendship. These differences were consistent with hypotheses derived from a family systems perspective.

Two Types of Close Friendships. Two types of friendships were found while observing pairs of close friends as they worked on a joint task: interdependent and disengaged. These types reflect different qualities of relationships at the dyadic level, which transcend the behavior of individuals. The interdependent friends cooperated on the task and respected each other's views and preferences. These close friends knew how to balance their closeness and individuality. Each of these dyads was connected by an emotional bond—it was important for them to cooperate. However, this closeness did not involve total dependence or preclude separate thoughts and actions. Closeness was coordinated with individuality (Youniss and Smollar, 1985). In the disengaged pairs, each partner emphasized individuality and separateness while working on the joint task. These close friends appeared incapable of restraining competition in order to act cooperatively. They did not tolerate differences of opinion and therefore worked separately, insisting on their individuality. This type of relationship recalls Howes's (1983) description of friends who are unable to sustain their connectedness in all circumstances. Although sincere closeness between friends is evident, it may "fade away" and later be resumed.

From a systems perspective, friendship types can be incorporated into a broader framework of families and relationships. These two types of friendship correspond to well-known family patterns (Constantine, 1987; Minuchin, 1974; Olson, Sprenkle, and Russel, 1979; Reiss, 1981; Wynne, 1958). For example, interdependent friends resemble environment-sensitive (Reiss, 1981) and clear-boundaries (Minuchin, 1974) families, and disengaged friends resemble distance-sensitive (Reiss, 1981) and disengaged (Minuchin, 1974) families.

The types of close friendships found in the present study also recall some of Karpel's (1976) modes of relationships. The interdependent type of friendship is similar to Karpel's dialogue stage of relationships. In this type of relationship, the poles of "I" and "we" are integrated in such a way that they nourish and foster each other. Individuation (the differentiated "I") and dialogue (the differentiated "we") are complementary parts of both partners' simultaneous self-delineation in the relationship. The more highly individuated the partners, the better prepared they are for a dialogue relationship. The disengaged type of friendship may represent a transitional, relational mode. In this mode, partners "maintain contact without fusion by establishing a pattern in which one partner keeps up a facade of distance, while the other pursues" (Karpel, 1976, p. 74). This type of interaction was clearly observed when disengaged adolescents worked on the joint task. Usually, one partner tried to initiate a consultation, while the other insisted on working separately.

Additional findings highlight the common ground of the two friendship types. Interdependent and disengaged pairs reported similar daily activities. They frequently met and spoke on the telephone, and their preferred topics of discussion were similar. They also pursued similar activities. These findings explain why both types of pairs perceived themselves and were perceived by others as close friends. Surface interactions in both types fulfilled needs of companionship and of mutual help and support (Berndt, 1986; Bukowski, Newcomb, and Hoza, 1987).

The distribution of close friendship types in early and middle adolescence suggests possible age-related differences in friendships. In early adolescence, only 39 percent of close friends in the sample were interdependent, whereas, in middle adolescence, 80 percent of close friends clearly preferred a greater degree of closeness and unity. This tendency probably reflects an increased need for a sense of shared intimacy with a close friend

(Sullivan, 1953; Sharabany, Gershoni, and Hofman, 1981). In early adolescence, intimacy involves self-reflection without strong interconnections to the partner's experiences (Selman, 1988). Hence, early adolescents do not yet have the need to commit themselves to truly cooperative relationships with their close friends.

The joint task may have contributed to these age-related differences, since some subjects felt competitive while working on the task. Competitive tasks can change the nature of interaction between close friends. Berndt (1987) found that fourth and sixth graders treated friends and classmates similarly when presented with a competitive task, but eighth graders preferred equality over competition with friends. With age, adolescents learn how to balance the needs of competition and closeness. This tendency was exhibited by the early adolescents in the present study who cooperated, though the majority appeared unable to balance the dyad's and the individuals' needs. For that reason, and in order to avoid conflict, these close friends preferred to work individually. With age and the growing need for mutual intimacy, there is a corresponding development of the ability to restrain competition and to establish interdependent close friendships.

Males and females were equally distributed across friendship types in both age cohorts, which argues against the notion of gender-based differences in the needs and perceptions of close friendships in adolescence. As Youniss and Smollar (1985, p. 127) reported, "Almost half of the males in any study [on friendship relationships] respond in identical fashion to the majority of females." At this time, any conclusions about gender-based differences in types of friendship are premature.

Friendship Reasoning and Cooperation Reasoning. Early adolescents who consulted and cooperated while working on the joint task revealed levels of friendship reasoning similar to those of adolescents who did not consult with their partners. But these cooperative early adolescents did exhibit a higher level of cooperation reasoning, probably because of their belief that friends should work together, in contrast to the uncooperative adolescents, who believed that it is more important to work individually. Although both friendship reasoning and cooperation reasoning are affected by the level of cognition, they are different. In the friendship reasoning task, adolescents reflected on a hypothetical question. Following the joint task, the cooperation reasoning question is not hypothetical but rather requires reflection on what the individual just experienced while working with a close friend. The early adolescents in this study may not have developed the cognitive ability to coordinate perspectives of self and other, and therefore their level of friendship reasoning was low and lacked mutuality. Reflection on current activities, however, does not require such advanced cognitive abilities (Main, Kaplan, and Cassidy, 1985).

Young adolescents probably have a tendency to cooperate (or not to cooperate) that is reflected in their behavior. Following Selman (1988,

p. 411), the capacity for mutual collaboration "is based on the developing ability to coordinate perspectives on the social interaction between the self and a significant other, in both a cognitive and an emotional sense," and "the ability to cooperate is demonstrated in both words and deeds, in thoughts and feeling" (p. 412). According to Freiberg (1969, p. 22), current experience may "revive mnemonic traces laid down through previous experience." Perhaps at a precognitive level a tendency to cooperate (or not to cooperate) exists and is expressed in both behavior and verbal explanations of behavior. It is probably much easier to instrumentally enact a certain tendency and reflect on it than to reason about hypothetical questions and the internal states of others (Hart, Ladd, and Burleson, 1990). With cognitive development during middle and late adolescence, social cognition becomes an additional factor that affects behavior.

For the sample of subjects in middle adolescence, disengaged dyads gave reasons for having a friend that were different from those expressed by interdependent dyads. Disengaged adolescents looked for a close friend to assuage loneliness and fulfill the need for intimacy. In addition, these dyads reported that a disagreement or fight can terminate a close friendship. Therefore, these adolescents sought to avoid stress on the relationship; they kept a certain distance to avoid differences of opinion and conflicts. Paradoxically, disengaged close friends preferred to be "distant" in order to preserve the closeness of their friendships.

Interdependent pairs' motivation for having a close friend reflected reasons usually found in studies on friendship: joint activities, willingness to help each other, and trust and intimacy (Berndt, 1986; Ginsburg, Gottman, and Parker, 1986; Hunter and Youniss, 1982; Sullivan, 1953). These middle adolescents did not look for a friend to overcome loneliness but instead sought friendship as an arena for personal growth. This motivation was especially evident when interdependent pairs were asked about the impact of strain on a relationship. They perceived jealousy and disagreement between friends as sources of change and development in the relationship. Interdependent pairs were capable of negotiating and balancing individuality and closeness. Disagreement was not a reason for termination of a friendship. Only in cases when mistrust compounded the relationship or the relationship lost the potential for self-growth was there a reason for termination of a friendship. Compared to disengaged pairs, interdependent pairs had more open and flexible relationships.

In both types of friendships, intimacy was clearly a reason for the establishment of a friendship. However, there are different kinds of intimacy (Selman, 1988). For example, in one type of intimacy, each partner reflects his or her own experience for the sake of self-satisfaction, without a strong sense of interconnecting experiences. In this case, intimacy reflects the sense that somebody is listening and that one is not alone. In another type of intimacy (of a higher level), partners incorporate each other's experiences and disclosures for a better mutual understanding of themselves and their relationship.

It is noteworthy that neither a consensus-sensitive (Reiss, 1981) nor an enmeshed (Minuchin, 1974) relationship was found among the types of close friendships in adolescence. Partners are very close to one another in an enmeshed relationship; consensus is important to them, and they suppress individual preferences to achieve greater closeness and unity. Although the need for intimacy motivates youngsters to establish close friendships, their levels of intimacy and commitment are not as strong as those in a family relationship.

The findings of the present study indicate that differences between the two types of close friendship are not clearly expressed in the common, daily activities of partners. More specific conditions, such as competition, highlight the distinctive nature of each type of relationship. Given the growing interest in the study of conflicts in friendship (Hartup, 1989), it would be interesting to determine whether interdependent and disengaged pairs differ in the nature of conflicts and modes of resolutions.

Different types of friendship revealed different levels of friendship reasoning. It may be that developmental differences (Selman, 1980) or heterogeneity in reasoning about friendship (Pellegrini, 1986) are related to the establishment of different types of close friendship. However, from a broader developmental perspective emphasizing continuity, it can be argued that different earlier patterns of relationships are carried forward (Sroufe and Fleeson, 1986) and expressed in the type of friendship established and in the level of friendship reasoning. Future studies, in which earlier relationships of adolescents are known, may illuminate the details of who establishes what type of close friendship in adolescence.

References

Berndt, T. J. "Social Cognition, Social Behavior, and Children's Friendship." In E. T. Higgins, D. N. Ruble, and W. W. Hartup (eds.), *Social Cognition and Social Development.* New York: Cambridge University Press, 1983.

Berndt, T. J. "Sharing Between Friends: Context and Consequences." In E. C. Mueller and C. R. Cooper (eds.), *Process and Outcome in Peer Relationships.* San Diego: Academic Press, 1986.

Berndt, T. J. "Prosocial Behavior Between Friends in Middle Childhood and Early Adolescence." *Journal of Early Adolescence,* 1987, 7, 307–317.

Bertalanffy, L. von. *General Systems Theory.* New York: Braziller, 1968.

Bigelow, B. J. "Children's Friendship Expectations: A Cognitive-Developmental Study." *Child Development,* 1977, 48, 247–253.

Blos, P. "The Second Individuation Process of Adolescence." In P. Blos (ed.), *The Adolescent Passage: Developmental Issues.* Madison, Conn.: International Universities Press, 1979. (Originally published 1967.)

Bukowski, W. M., Newcomb, A. F., and Hoza, B. "Friendship Conceptions Among Early

Adolescents: A Longitudinal Study of Stability and Change." *Journal of Early Adolescence,* 1987, *7,* 143–152.

Charlesworth, W. R., and LaFreniere, P. "Dominance, Friendship, and Resource Utilization in Preschool Children's Groups." *Ethology and Sociobiology,* 1983, *4,* 175–186.

Constantine, L. L. "Adolescence Process and Family Organization: A Model of Development as a Function of Family Paradigm." *Journal of Adolescent Research,* 1987, *2,* 349–366.

Freiberg, S. "Libidinol, Object Constancy, and Mental Representation." *Psychoanalytic Study of the Child,* 1969, *24,* 9–47.

Furman, W., and Bierman, K. L. "Developmental Changes in Young Children's Conceptions of Friendship." *Child Development,* 1983, *54,* 549–556.

Ginsberg, D., Gottman, J. M., and Parker, J. G. "The Importance of Friendship." In J. M. Gottman and J. G. Parker (eds.), *Conversations of Friends.* New York: Cambridge University Press, 1986.

Gottman, J. M., and Mettetal, G. "Speculation About Social and Affective Development: Friendship and Acquaintanceship Through Adolescence." In J. M. Gottman and J. G. Parker (eds.), *Conversations of Friends.* New York: Cambridge University Press, 1986.

Hart, C. H., Ladd, G. W., and Burleson, B. R. "Children's Expectations of Social Strategies: Relations with Sociometric Status and Maternal Disciplinary Styles." *Child Development,* 1990, *41,* 127–137.

Hartup, W. W. "Peer Relations." In E. M. Hetherington (ed.), *Handbook of Child Psychology.* Vol. 4: *Socialization, Personality, and Social Development.* New York: Wiley, 1983.

Hartup, W. W. "On Relationships and Development." In W. W. Hartup and Z. Rubin (eds.), *Relationships and Development.* Hillsdale, N.J.: Erlbaum, 1986.

Hartup, W. W. "Behavioral Manifestations of Children's Friendships." In T. J. Berndt and G. W. Ladd (eds.), *Peer Relationships in Child Development.* New York: Wiley, 1989.

Hartup, W. W., Laursen, B., Stewart, M., and Eastenson, A. "Conflict and the Friendship Relations of Young Children." *Child Development,* 1988, *59,* 1590–1600.

Hinde, R. A. *Towards Understanding Relationships.* London: Academic Press, 1979.

Howes, C. "Patterns of Friendship." Paper presented at the biennial meeting of the Society for Research in Child Development, Boston, Apr. 1981.

Howes, C. "Patterns of Friendship." *Child Development,* 1983, *54,* 1041–1053.

Hunter, F. T., and Youniss, J. "Changes in Functions of Three Relations During Adolescence." *Developmental Psychology,* 1982, *18,* 806–811.

Karpel, M. "Individuation: From Fusion to Dialogue." *Family Process,* 1976, *15,* 65–82.

Keller, N., and Wood, P. "Development of Friendship Reasoning: A Study of Inter-Individual Differences in Intra-Individual Change." *Developmental Psychology,* 1989, *25,* 820–826.

Main, M., Kaplan, N. E., and Cassidy, J. "Security in Infancy, Childhood, and Adulthood: A Move to the Level of Representation." In I. Bretherton and E. Waters (eds.), *Growing Points of Attachment: Theory and Research.* Monographs of the Society for Research in Child Development, vol. 50, nos. 1–2 (serial no. 209). Chicago: University of Chicago Press, 1985.

Minuchin, S. *Family and Family Therapy.* Cambridge, Mass.: Harvard University Press, 1974.

Newcomb, A. F., and Brady, J. E. "Mutuality in Boys' Friendship Relations." *Child Development,* 1982, *53,* 392–395.

Oden, S., Hertzberger, S. D., Mangaine, P. L., and Wheeler, V. A. "Children's Peer Relationships: An Examination of Social Processes." In J. C. Masters and K. Yarkin-Levin (eds.), *Boundary Areas in Social and Developmental Psychology.* San Diego: Academic Press, 1984.

Olson, D. H., Sprenkle, D., and Russel, C. "Circumplex Model of Marital and Family Systems. Part 1: Cohesion and Adaptability Dimensions, Family Types, and Clinical Application." *Family Process,* 1979, *18,* 3–28.

Pellegrini, D. S. "Variability in Children's Level of Reasoning About Friendship." *Journal of Applied Developmental Psychology,* 1986, *7,* 341–354.

Reiss, D. *The Family's Construction of Reality*. Cambridge, Mass.: Harvard University Press, 1981.

Selman, R. L. *The Growth of Interpersonal Understanding: Developmental and Clinical Analyses*. San Diego: Academic Press, 1980.

Selman, R. L. "Fostering Intimacy and Autonomy." In W. Damon (ed.), *Child Development Today and Tomorrow*. San Francisco: Jossey-Bass, 1988.

Selman, R. L., and Jacquette, D. "Stability and Oscillation in Inter-Personal Awareness: A Clinical Developmental Analysis." In C. B. Keasey (ed.), *Social Cognitive Development*. Nebraska Symposium on Motivation, vol. 25. Lincoln: University of Nebraska Press, 1977.

Sharabany, R., Gershoni, R., and Hofman, J. E. "Girlfriend, Boyfriend: Age and Sex Differences in Intimate Friendship." *Developmental Psychology*, 1981, *17*, 800–808.

Sroufe, L. A., and Fleeson, J. "Attachment and the Construction of Relationships." In W. W. Hartup and Z. Rubin (eds.), *Relationships and Development*. Hillsdale, N.J.: Erlbaum, 1986.

Steinglass, P. "The Conceptualization of Marriage from a System Theory Perspective." In T. J. Paulino and B. S. McGrady (eds.), *Marriage and Marital Therapy*. New York: Brunner/ Mazel, 1978.

Sullivan, H. S. *The Interpersonal Theory of Psychiatry*. New York: Norton, 1953.

Wright, P. H. "Self-Referent Motivation and the Intrinsic Quality of Friendship." *Journal of Social and Personal Relationships*, 1984, *1*, 115–130.

Wynne, L. C. "Pseudomutuality in the Families of Schizophrenics." *Psychiatry*, 1958, *21*, 205–250.

Wynne, L. C. "Communication Disorders and the Quest for Relatedness in Families of Schizophrenics." *American Journal of Psychoanalysis*, 1970, *30*, 100–114.

Youniss, J. *Parents and Peers in Social Development: A Piaget-Sullivan Perspective*. Chicago: University of Chicago Press, 1980.

Youniss, J., and Smollar, J. *Adolescent Relations with Mothers, Fathers, and Friends*. Chicago: University of Chicago Press, 1985.

SHMUEL SHULMAN is in the Department of Psychology at Bar-Ilan University, Ramat Gan, Israel. His main interests are adolescent development and family systems and therapy.

*Adolescents prefer close intimate friendships with real same-sex
friends as compared to imaginary companions. The developmental
benefits of both types of relationships are analyzed, stressing
emotional needs, social support, and coping assistance.*

Close Friendship and Imaginary Companions in Adolescence

Inge Seiffge-Krenke

For many adolescents, relations with friends are critical interpersonal
bridges to psychological growth and social maturity (Savin-Williams and
Berndt, 1990). Moreover, in construing friendship as an indication of
healthiness and social maturity, parents worry if their children do not have
close friends (Achenbach and Edelbrock, 1981). In this chapter, I analyze
the developmental significance of close friendship, covering the emotional
and social needs that these relationships meet and the support that they
provide to adolescents. More specifically, I analyze the function of close
friends as coping models in the transition from adolescence to adulthood.

Mainly, I draw on attachment theory as a conceptual framework for
analyzing both real friendship behavior and imaginary companionship.
Two major questions are addressed. First, is the imaginary companion a
substitute for family and friends? In other words, are adolescents with a
deficit in intimacy and companionship especially likely to construct imaginary companions? Second, what can be said about the quality and significance of close friendships that are established and maintained alongside
imaginary companions?

Theoretical Framework: Attachment Theory

Family relations are altered in the course of adolescence, and the role of
friendships as a source of activities, influence, and support increases

This investigation was completed with support from Deutsche Forschungs-gemeinschaft,
DFG, Grant Se 408, 1-3.

dramatically. According to Sullivan (1953), friends serve several related functions. They offer consensual validation of interests, hopes, and fears, bolster feelings of self-worth, and provide affection and opportunities for intimate disclosure. In addition, friends promote the growth of interpersonal sensitivity and serve as prototypes for later romantic, marital, and parental relationships. Similarly, Hartup and Sancilio (1986) listed three friendship functions: sources of emotional security and support, contexts for growth in social competence, and prototypes for later relationships.

Research on adolescent relationships with family and friends has demonstrated important links between these two socialization contexts, although compared to their other attachments, adolescents' friendships are less exclusive and more equitable in the distribution of power (Hartup, 1983). According to Blos (1967), the second individuation process in adolescence resembles early attachments. Close personal relationships have similar psychological functions throughout life. They may differ in form and surface representations, but fundamentally they are similar processes. Bowlby (1979) emphasized that the early relationship with the caregiver is a model for later relationships, shaping expectations and beliefs about oneself and others, especially in new situations (Bretherton and Waters, 1985).

Although there is a growing interest in extending the study of attachment beyond early childhood (Greenberg, Siegel, and Leitch, 1983; Kahn and Antonucci, 1980), little is known about intimate attachment in adolescence (Hill, 1987). Working representations of the self and others may be viewed as momentarily activated schemas reflecting current situational cues and the person's developmental history (Westen and others, 1991). Although the adolescent may become detached (the orthodox view) or individuated (the contemporary view) from his or her parents, this occurs before the young person has developed an internal structure to function autonomously. But little research has been done on internal representation and the symbolic construction of adolescent relationships, a framework that clarifies behavior previously considered inexplicable, puzzling, or even irrational.

Imaginary Companions. In the psychoanalytic framework, different constructs of independence have been developed. Winnicott's (1953) concept of transitional object keeps inner and outer reality separate yet interrelated. It represents aspects of the mother that enable a child to cope with separation anxiety at a stage when object constancy has not yet been reached (Bretherton and Waters, 1985). Although mostly observed in childhood, the transitional object may also fulfill the need for intimacy and affiliation in adolescence (see Lundy and Potts, 1987; Blos, 1967). An imaginary companion represents a specific type of transitional object. Defined as "an invisible, name bearing person who presents for the constructor a psychic reality over an extended period of time" (Svendsen,

1934, p. 985), the imaginary companion is distinct from imaginative play (Partington and Grant, 1984). It is unclear whether the imaginary companion proceeds developmentally as a continuation of transitional objects in toddlerhood (see, for example, Benson, 1980).

There are two main approaches to imaginary companions, one reflecting the psychoanalytic tradition and the other incorporating assumptions and methods of developmental psychology. Psychoanalytic authors investigate imaginary companions primarily through intense case studies of children (Nagera, 1969). Until recently, psychoanalytic authors focused on conflict-reducing functions, where the imaginary companion is interpreted as a vehicle either for discharging unacceptable impulses (Freud, [1936] 1966; Burlingham, 1945; Sperling, 1954) or for prolonging feelings of omnipotence (Bach, 1971; Fraiberg, 1959). In particular, compensatory functions were emphasized. Several authors demonstrated that imaginary companions appear when the mother is pregnant with another child (Benson and Pryor, 1973) and gives birth to a sibling (Burlingham, 1945), when the mother is absent due to frequent hospitalization (Myers, 1979), when the mother, father, or another caregiver dies (Bach, 1971; Benson, 1980), when parents divorce, or when a friend is lost (Benson and Pryor, 1973; Nagera, 1969). Feelings of loneliness, neglect, and rejection were thus seen to motivate a person to create imaginary companions. Currently, psychoanalytic research on imaginary companions (see, for example, Benson, 1980; Rucker, 1981) emphasizes positive developmental features such as coping and adjustment functions: "In the absence of gross pathology, a child who invents an imaginary friend is able to use his own strengths to cope with stress in a way that interferes minimally with the accomplishment of age appropriate tasks" (Rucker, 1981, p. 136).

Relatively little research on imaginary companions has been undertaken by developmental psychologists (Masih, 1978; Partington and Grant, 1984). Typically, large samples of normal subjects have been studied by interviewing the children or their parents retrospectively. The findings have been contradictory with respect to incidence (Bender and Vogel, 1941; Hurlock and Burstein, 1932) and age groups who construct imaginary companions (Piaget, 1951; Bender and Vogel, 1941; Schaefer, 1969). With respect to gender and birth order, the results have been more consistent: The incidence of imaginary companions is higher among girls than boys (Masterson, 1975), and among firstborn or only children (Hurlock, 1968; Svendsen, 1934; Manosewitz, Prentice, and Wilson, 1973). These empirical studies support the compensatory function hypothesis, which was also stressed in the early psychoanalytic work. Other studies support the view that imaginary companions provide mental rehearsal for social development (for example, Svendsen, 1934; Schaefer, 1969; Singer and Singer, 1981). This view was articulated by Piaget (1951), who commented on the imaginary companion of his daughter Jacqueline: "This strange creature which engaged her attention for about two months was help in all that she learned or devised, gave her moral encouragement in obeying orders and consoled her when she was unhappy. Then it disappeared" (p. 130).

Close Friendship. The help of "very special friends" may be especially appreciated in adolescence. The transition to adulthood is difficult, not only because of pubertal changes (Tobin-Richards, Boxer, and Petersen, 1983) but also because of complex and interrelated developmental tasks such as disengaging from the family, developing an occupational identity, or establishing a heterosexual relationship. Several authors have stressed that adolescents perceive friendship as a supportive relationship (for example, Berndt and Perry, 1986) and that friends provide new perspectives from which adolescents discover their own power to co-construct ideas and receive validation (for example, Youniss and Smollar, 1985). As mentioned earlier, adolescents' friendships differ from their other attachments in that they are less exclusive and more equitable in the distribution of power. This implies that adolescents learn about themselves from friendship, especially about aspects that are barred from their relationships with parents owing to fear of judgment and need for approval. Research on privacy and self-disclosure confirms this view (Laufer and Wolfe, 1974; Broughton, 1981), as do findings pointing to the importance of friends for coping assistance (Seiffge-Krenke, 1992). In fact, studies using interviews, questionnaires, and observational data have consistently indicated that adolescents emphasize reciprocal disclosure, intimate sharing, and social support as salient criteria of close friendship (Selman, 1980; Berndt, 1981; Parker and Gottman, 1989).

Among all changes, the increased intimacy of adolescent friendship has been given the most attention (Buhrmester, 1990; Buhrmester and Furman, 1987; Craig-Bray and Adams, 1986) and is most often treated as the prototypical feature of adolescent friendship, especially among girls. As Furman and Robbins (1985) indicated, these relationships involve mutual activities, self-disclosure, and reciprocal feelings of satisfaction. The benefits of close friendship also depend on similarity among friends (Savin-Williams and Berndt, 1990). From midadolescence onward, parents are replaced by coevals as trustworthy partners in personally relevant experiences and events (Rivenbark, 1971; Andersen and Ross, 1984). With parents, adolescents typically talk about school and career goals; with friends, they talk about dating, sexuality, and personal experiences, interests, and aims.

The importance of friendship is reflected in the increased amounts of daily free time spent in activities with friends and in talking with friends (Crockett, Losoff, and Petersen, 1984; Buhrmester and Furman, 1987). Moreover, greater social support seeking and improved social comparison processes point to the growing function of friends as coping models (Seiffge-Krenke, 1992).

Several authors have described gender differences in friendship development. Females experience intimacy in same-sex friendship earlier than males (Douvan and Adelson, 1966), report greater intimacy in friendship (Sharabany, Gershoni, and Hofman, 1981), maintain a smaller number of friends, and are less willing to expand a dyadic relationship to include a third person (Buhrmester and Furman, 1987). Males tend to deemphasize the affective components of friendships and to stress the instrumental aspects, for example, close friends support each other in times of trouble.

Youths who do not have intimate friendships miss out on important validation interactions and are deprived of social support and coping assistance. Are these adolescents therefore especially likely to construct imaginary companions? Are fantasy constructs attractive interlocution partners in the complex and vaguely defined transition to adulthood? Are they even more attractive than coeval friends because self-related information and secrecy are easier to manipulate? My research was designed to answer these questions, focusing mainly on the quality of adolescents' relationships with imaginary companions and close friends. Two converging lines of thought from attachment theory and developmental research—the deficit hypothesis and the coping hypothesis—constituted the theoretical framework of the research. Although the lines of thought are related, each distinctively contributes to an understanding of close friendships in adolescence.

Data Base

Past research on friendships and their functions has relied mainly on questionnaires and interviews with adolescents, or, more rarely, on observations of friendship interaction. Studies of imaginary companionship have used retrospective methods and reports from individuals familiar with the adolescents in the subject samples. We conducted two studies utilizing interviews and questionnaires about friendship as well as adolescents' written representations of their social world in diaries. Diary writing was chosen as a data source because it is a youth-typical activity especially frequent among females (Seiffge-Krenke, in press). Because the adolescent diary is not written for a particular addressee, we assumed that the descriptions of relationships were unaltered and honest and represented the specific point of view of the writer at the time of the entry. In both studies, we compared the data from diary writers with the data from age-mates who did not keep diaries.

Study 1. The first study was designed to answer the following questions: How frequent are imaginary companions in different age groups? Which adolescents construct imaginary companions, and does this choice covary with a deficit in relationships with close friends? What are the characteristics of the imaginary companions as described by the adolescents?

A total of 241 adolescents (112 males and 129 females), attending grades six through eleven in German comprehensive schools, participated in the study. The adolescents were predominantly from lower- and upper-middle-class families. In this sample, 94 adolescents (80 females and 14 males) kept diaries. This subgroup did not differ from the remaining subjects in sociodemographic traits and family structure. Moreover, there were no differences between the adolescent diarists and age-mates who did not keep diaries in total numbers of friends. Overall, girls reported fewer close friends than were reported by boys (M's = 1.2 and 2.3, respectively).

The diarists were interviewed about their motives for and duration of diary keeping, modes of secrecy, diary contents (persons and situations dealt with in the diary), and, if applicable, any special traits of the imaginary companion (for example, age, gender, appearance, and life situation). A content analysis of the diary-keeping and imaginary companion activities was carried out by two independent judges. Concordance coefficients (kappa) for the twelve content categories ranged from .68 to .81. Before the interview, each subject completed several questionnaires assessing self-concept (Seiffge-Krenke, 1987), role-taking ability (Feffer, 1970), readiness to disclose (Koch, 1977), coping behavior (Seiffge-Krenke, 1989b), and egocentrism (Elkind and Bowen, 1979); the adolescents also were asked to specify the frequency of their daydreams per week (for details on the instruments and procedures, see Seiffge-Krenke, in press).

Study 2. In the second study, the relationship between imaginary companionship and close friendship behavior was investigated. A group of diarists was interviewed and their diary contents analyzed in order to answer the following questions: How frequently are imaginary companions mentioned in the diaries? What are the characteristics of the imaginary companions described in the entries? How are relationships with close friends described in the diaries?

The basic material for this study consisted of forty diaries written by twenty adolescents (three males and seventeen females). A sample of entries was drawn from this material for closer examination by content analysis (for details, see Seiffge-Krenke, 1992). Each subject answered an extensive battery of questionnaires covering role taking, egocentrism, self-concept, self-disclosure, and coping strategies, as described above for the first study. The subjects who allowed us to use their diaries for content analysis were in the transition period between late adolescence and adulthood (M = 21.6 years), representing a broad occupational spectrum. Eleven of the twenty subjects had a stable relationship with a partner. The average duration for keeping a diary was five years, beginning between the ages of eleven and thirteen.

To standardize the texts, eighty entries over two consecutive years were analyzed for each writer. The content analysis used sixty categories: eight on text features (such as length, greetings, colloquial style, and reference to self-disclosure) and five on imaginary companions (such as incidence, traits, and quality of relationship with writer). The other forty-seven content categories were collapsed into sixteen main categories such as work, school, conflicts, and close friendships. Two independent judges categorized the material; their average rates of agreement (kappa) over all categories and subjects ranged between .64 and .72. In the analysis of close friendships, only female diarists were included.

Adolescents Who Constructed Imaginary Companions

In our interviews, we found that diary keeping started in early adolescence, reached its peak in midadolescence, and lost its attraction thereafter. The reported reasons for keeping a diary included fashion, memory prop, chance, and a missing confidant. Lack of a trustworthy communication partner was mentioned only by female diarists: For 23 percent of the female diarists, this was the reason for starting a diary.

To determine which variables best predicted construction of an imaginary companion, a stepwise multiple-regression analysis was carried out. The twelve predictor variables included self-concept scales, coping scales, and scales for self-disclosure, role-taking ability, egocentrism, and daydreaming. Dependent variables included incidence and traits (age, gender, and appearance) of imaginary companions described in the diary entries.

Table 5.1 shows that readiness for daydreaming represented the most powerful predictor, followed by active coping strategies (such as asking others for advice or help). Self-concept, especially positive self-esteem, also made a significant contribution. Role-taking ability and self-disclosure readiness were included in the stepwise multiple-regression analysis, even though their power of prediction was only tangential. Apparently, these adolescents were ready to tackle problems in exchanges with interaction

Table 5.1. Prediction of Imaginary Companions in Diaries

Variable/ Step	Predictor	F	Beta	Multiple R	R
1	Daydreaming	5.6[a]	.46	.36	.26
2	Coping scale 1: Active coping by means of social resources	3.8[a]	.44	.45	.26
3	Self-concept scale 1: Positive self-esteem	2.8[b]	.41	.53	.24
4	Role taking	2.5[b]	.49	.59	.15
5	Self-disclosure	2.2[b]	.58	.67	.11

Note: N = 94.

[a] $p < .01$

[b] $p < .10$

Source: Based on Seiffge-Krenke, 1992, in press.

partners, whether real or imaginary. Two sides of the exchanges were evidenced: empathy with the partner and openness.

Imaginary Companions in Diaries

One-half of the female diarists, but only one-third of the male diarists, in Study 1 reported imaginary companions. A content analysis showed similarities and differences in appearance ("He is taller than I am"), characteristic traits ("She is more understanding than I am"), and life situation ("She is financially better off") between the adolescent and the imaginary companion. Both genders more frequently chose female imaginary companions, who in general resembled the writers. The imaginary companions, like the diarists, seemed to pass through different stages of change over the years. They became impersonal and, finally, were hardly mentioned any longer by older diarists. The fourteen- and fifteen-year-olds had the most reports of imaginary companions.

In analyzing diary entries in Study 2, we again found evidence of imaginary companions. A female diarist, fifteen years old, described her imaginary companion in one diary entry as follows:

> Who is Kathrin?? What does Kathrin mean to me?
>
> Kathrin is an amiable girl who moves gracefully. She is very pretty when she is happy. She has the most beautiful dark-brown eyes I have ever seen, for they are incredibly expressive—sometimes like stars, sometimes like the dead sea: so deep and calm and sadly wide. Yet that is but what a friend can seize from outside. Sure, through her eyes I can see right into her, but still I know very little about her real inner life. I do not even know what her relationship with God is really like—my ideas may be so mistaken.
>
> What else is Kathrin?
>
> Intelligent, ambitious, affectionate, helpful, sometimes a bit hard to understand, sometimes she mothers everybody, but all that is just her— without it, she would not be Kathrin. There are times when I have the impression that she could do everything perfectly and then I am almost relieved when I discover a fault. Moreover she is quite taciturn and it takes her a long time before she is able to confide in somebody, she seems to settle a lot just between herself and God, to whom she seems to completely hold fast. I can describe her—but who is she really? How long will it take me to come a single millimeter closer to the right answer . . . ?!?

In some diaries, the imaginary companions were introduced at the beginning, with precise descriptions of personal characteristics and other traits. Other diarists give less explicit descriptions of their imaginary companions. They added questions and comments after descriptions of certain events or experiences, inviting the imaginary companions to take up the writer's position, to criticize or evaluate the writer's life-style, philosophy, or habits, or to add experiences. The construction of imaginary companions was reported by 35 percent of the eleven- to thirteen-year-olds, 55 percent of the fourteen- to fifteen-year-olds, and 28 percent of the sixteen- to seventeen-year-olds. The existence of an imaginary companion was correlated with text features such as greetings (biserial correlation coefficient r_b = .59), farewells (r_b = .68), sequential dialogue (r_b = .41), self-disclosure references (r_b = .39), and communicative writing (r_b = .35).

Dimensions of Close Friendship

The content of the diaries covered a broad range of topic categories. Focusing only on female subjects' diaries, we found that self and others, that is, the diarist and her social relationships, were the main themes in 70 percent of all entries. Close friendship, social comparison, empathetic reflections about significant others, and heterosexual relationships also were important. Descriptions and evaluations of the self, school, and work were less important.

Close friendship between girls was mentioned in 38 percent of all entries. How were relationships with close friends described in the diaries? We found that dyadic relationships were the preferred form of close friendship between girls; whereas triads were mentioned less often. The activities named in descriptions of leisure time, leisure places, and friendship interactions indicated that the diarists spent more time with other females (M = 46 activities) than with males (M = 17 activities). There were five different categories of joint activities: (1) doing things together (for example, chores, homework, and shopping) was named by 19 percent; (2) intimate, symbiotic, or homoerotic activities (for example, changing clothes, staying in the bathroom together, applying makeup, and holding hands) were mentioned by 45 percent; (3) norm breaking (for example, taking drugs and stealing) was mentioned by less than 5 percent; and (4) symbolic or (5) actual approaches to the opposite sex (for example, fantasizing about boys, making plans to meet them, writing love letters, and double dating) were mentioned by 22 percent and 10 percent, respectively (see Figure 5.1).

The diarists make more comments on peers (48 percent) than on adults (19 percent), and they compared themselves more often to peers (18 percent) than to adults (4 percent). We found that intimate activities between close friends related to the body, external appearance, and female roles; proximity and close body contact were frequent. The symbolic approach to males centered on fantasies, wishful thinking, and potential encounters, whereas the actual approach involved contacts, mainly under

Figure 5.1. Percentage Distribution of
Close Friendship Activities Shared by Female Diarists

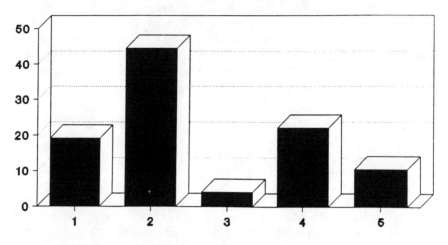

Note: 1 = doing things together, 2 = intimate, symbiotic, or homoerotic activities, 3 = norm breaking, 4 = symbolic approach to the opposite sex, 5 = actual approach to the opposite sex

Source: Based on Seiffge-Krenke, in press.

the protection of the same-sex friend. The first contacts with romantic partners were characterized by physical distance, with the same-sex friend serving a fear-reducing and protective function. Romantic relationships with intimacy and closeness were mentioned in 19 percent of the diaries.

When the group of diarists was divided into writers with ($N = 10$) and without ($N = 10$) an imaginary companion, only slight differences between the groups were found. Diarists with an imaginary companion reported significantly less about work ($\chi^2 = 5.9, p < .01$), school ($\chi^2 = 5.0, p < .02$), and heterosexual relationships ($\chi^2 = 4.9, p < .03$) but significantly more about "how others see me" ($\chi^2 = 12.8, p < .001$). Adolescents with and without an imaginary companion did not differ with respect to the frequency of intimate, symbiotic activities, or activities involving the opposite sex.

Conclusion

Drawing predominantly from attachment theory, I have outlined protective functions of close friendships in adolescence. Two major benefits were emphasized: fulfillment of emotional needs for closeness and intimacy, and social support and coping assistance. The review of empirical research in developmental psychology and psychoanalytic case studies converged on two hypotheses about the functions of imaginary companions: to compensate for a lack of close friends and to cope with developmental needs during the period of transition from adolescence to adulthood.

Generally, these results demonstrate the benefits of close relationships, whether real or imaginary. These relationships provide consensual validation, social support, and coping assistance, particularly against potential stressors (such as body changes, sexuality, and dating) that adolescents cannot comfortably discuss with parents (see Buhrmester and Furman, 1987). In our research, one of the best predictors of imaginary companions—readiness for active coping by means of social resources—supports psychoanalytic and developmental research emphasizing positive growth and coping functions (Benson, 1980; Rucker, 1981; Partington and Grant, 1984).

Our results do not support the deficit hypothesis: Adolescents with an imaginary companion did not have a deficit in social interaction. Indeed, diarists with and without an imaginary companion did not differ with respect to either family structure or the number and closeness of friends. Dyadic relationships with same-sex peers were preferred in both groups, and the frequency of reported intimacy, closeness, and modeling behavior between friends was comparable. In addition, the criteria for friendship with an imaginary companion resembled those for close friendship in real life. Role-taking ability and perspective coordination were also high among the adolescents with an imaginary companion.

Sullivan (1953) hypothesized that adolescents' intimacy and sensitivity with same-sex friends transfers to relationships with opposite-sex friends. Our results illustrate that close friendships uniquely contribute to the development of social competence and help to prepare adolescents for romantic love. Close friends assist each other in matters of sexual and personal identity by mirroring and shaping behavior on a very concrete level, for example, with respect to clothing, hairstyle, interests, leisure activities, and dating. Given the frequency with which close friendship behavior was mentioned in the diaries of our subjects and the broad variety of activities in same-sex dyads that was described, the diarists clearly were concerned about and active with their best friends. These findings support the arguments of Buhrmester and Furman (1987) and Sharabany, Gershoni, and Hofman (1981), who demonstrated the special significance of intimacy in girls' close friendship. Our results also support the findings of Berndt and Hoyle (1985) on the exclusivity of female friendships.

The behaviors, activities, and reflections reported in the diaries answer the question "Who am I?" The diary entries made clear that this process of self-definition is a central theme in close friendships. Discussion of similarities and differences of others were frequent in the diaries, especially in regard to relations with imaginary companions.

Apparently, imaginary companions are not constructed "when friends fall out" (Benson and Pryor, 1973, p. 457). But they do not provide much coping assistance compared to real friends. What, then, are the developmental benefits of imaginary companions? One advantage is that closeness, intimacy, and self-disclosure are controlled by the diarist, protecting him or her from narcissistic injuries and conflict. Another advantage is that interaction with the imaginary companion elaborates similarities and differences between the diarist and his or her imaginary companion, underscoring the relational definition of self (Damon and Hart, 1982). The imaginary companion is thus restricted to mirroring the self and is of no direct significance in the transition to romantic relationships.

Even with the high incidence of imaginary companionship, adolescents prefer intense relationships with close real friends. In a follow-up study (see Seiffge-Krenke, in press), we found that imaginary companions and close friendship behavior are given up when heterosexual relationships begin. By midadolescence, the body has physically changed, but a definite and new sex role has not yet formed. Our findings describe an active restructuring of self while relationships with imaginary and close real friends are maintained. Conceptually, both imaginary companionship and close friendship behavior help adolescents cope with the challenges of the transition to romantic relationships, providing emotional support and minimizing conflict. Consequently, both lose significance when the restructuring of identity and relationships is completed.

References

Achenbach, T. M., and Edelbrock, C. S. *Behavioral Problems and Competencies Reported by Parents of Normal and Disturbed Children.* Monographs of the Society for Research in Child Development, vol. 46, no. 1 (serial no. 188). Chicago: University of Chicago Press, 1981.

Andersen, S. M., and Ross, I. "Self-Knowledge and Social Inference: The Diagnosticity of Cognitive, Affective, and Behavioral Data." *Journal of Personality and Social Psychology,* 1984, *46,* 280–293.

Bach, S. "Notes on Some Imaginary Companions." *Psychoanalytic Study of the Child,* 1971, *26,* 159–171.

Bandura, A. "The Stormy Decade: Fact or Fiction?" *Psychology in the Schools,* 1964, *3,* 224–231.

Bender, L., and Vogel, B. F. "Imaginary Companions of Children." *American Journal of Orthopsychiatry,* 1941, *11,* 56–65.

Benson, R. M. "Narcissistic Guardians: Developmental Aspects of Transitional Objects, Imaginary Companions, and Career Fantasies." *Adolescent Psychiatry,* 1980, *8,* 253–264.

Benson, R. M., and Pryor, D. B. " 'When Friends Fall Out': Developmental Interference with the Function of Some Imaginary Companions." *Journal of the American Psychoanalytic Association,* 1973, *21,* 457–473.

Berndt, T. J. "Developmental Changes in Conformity to Peers and Parents." *Developmental Psychology,* 1979, *15,* 608–616.

Berndt, T. J. "Relations Between Social Cognition, Nonsocial Cognition, and Social Behavior: The Case of Friendship." In J. H. Flavell and L. Ross (eds.), *Social Cognitive Development: Frontiers and Possible Futures.* Cambridge, England: Cambridge University Press, 1981.

Berndt, T. J., and Hoyle, S. G. "Stability and Change in Childhood and Adolescent Friendships." *Developmental Psychology,* 1985, *21,* 1007–1015.

Berndt, T. J., and Perry, T. B. "Children's Perceptions of Friendships as Supportive Relationships." *Developmental Psychology,* 1986, *22,* 640–648.

Blos, P. "The Second Individuation Process of Adolescence." *Psychoanalytic Study of the Child,* 1967, *22,* 162–186.

Bowlby, J. "Separation and Loss Within the Family." In J. Bowlby (ed.), *The Making and Breaking of Affectional Bonds.* London: Tavistock, 1979.

Bretherton, I., and Waters, E. (eds.). *Growing Points of Attachment: Theory and Research.* Monographs of the Society for Research in Child Development, vol. 50, nos. 1–2 (serial no. 209). Chicago: University of Chicago Press, 1985.

Broughton, J. M. "The Divided Self in Adolescence." *Human Development,* 1981, *24,* 13–32.

Buhrmester, D. "Intimacy of Friendship, Interpersonal Competence, and Adjustment During Preadolescence and Adolescence." *Child Development,* 1990, *61,* 1101–1111.

Buhrmester, D., and Furman, W. "The Development of Companionship and Intimacy." *Child Development,* 1987, *58,* 1101–1113.

Burlingham, D. "The Fantasy of Having a Twin." *Psychoanalytic Study of the Child,* 1945, *1,* 205–210.

Craig-Bray, L., and Adams, G. R. "Measuring Social Intimacy in Same-Sex and Opposite-Sex Contexts." *Journal of Adolescent Research,* 1986, *1,* 95–101.

Crockett, L., Losoff, M., and Petersen, A. C. "Perception of the Peer Group and Friendship in Early Adolescence." *Journal of Early Adolescence,* 1984, *4,* 155–181.

Damon, W., and Hart, D. "The Development of Self-Understanding from Infancy Through Adolescence." *Child Development,* 1982, *53,* 841–864.

Douvan, E., and Adelson, J. *The Adolescent Experience.* New York: Wiley, 1966.

Elkind, D., and Bowen, R. "Imaginary Audience Behavior in Children and Adolescents." *Developmental Psychology,* 1979, *15,* 38–44.

Feffer, M. "A Developmental Analysis of Interpersonal Behavior." *Psychological Review,* 1970, *77,* 197–214.

Fraiberg, S. *The Magic Years.* New York: Charles Scribner's Sons, 1959.

Freud, A. *The Ego and the Mechanisms of Defense.* (Rev. ed.) Madison, Conn.: International Universities Press, 1966. (Originally published 1936.)

Furman, W., and Robbins, P. "What's the Point? Issues in the Selection of Treatment Objectives." In B. H. Schneider, K. H. Rubin, and J. E. Ledingham (eds.), *Children's Peer Relations: Issues in Assessment and Intervention.* New York: Springer-Verlag, 1985.

Greenberg, M. T., Siegel, J. M., and Leitch, C. J. "The Nature and Importance of Attachment Relationships to Parents and Peers During Adolescence." *Journal of Youth and Adolescence,* 1983, *12,* 373–386.

Hartup, W. W. "Peer Relations." In E. M. Hetherington (ed.), *Handbook of Child Psychology.* Vol. 4: *Socialization, Personality, and Social Development.* New York: Wiley, 1983.

Hartup, W. W., and Sancilio, M. F. "Children's Friendships." In E. Schopler and G. B. Mesibov (eds.), *Social Behavior in Autism.* New York: Plenum, 1986.

Hazan, C., and Shaver, P. "Romantic Love Conceptualized as an Attachment Process." *Journal of Personality and Social Psychology,* 1987, *52,* 511–524.

Hill, J. P. "Research on Adolescents and Their Families: Past and Prospect." In C. E. Irwin, Jr. (ed.), *Adolescent Social Behavior and Health.* New Directions for Child Development, no. 37. San Francisco: Jossey-Bass, 1987.

Hurlock, E. B. *Child Growth and Development.* (3rd ed.) New York: McGraw-Hill, 1968.

Hurlock, E. B., and Burstein, M. "The Imaginary Playmate: A Questionnaire Study." *Journal of Genetic Psychology,* 1932, *41,* 380–392.

Kahn, R. L., and Antonucci, T. C. "Convoys Over the Life Course: Attachment, Roles, and Social Support." In P. B. Baltes and O. G. Brim (eds.), *Life Span Development and Behavior.* Vol. 3. San Diego: Academic Press, 1980.

Koch, S. J. "The Interest and Concerns of Adolescents, Grades Seven Through Twelve, as Expressed in Their Written Compositions." *Dissertation Abstracts International,* 1977, *37,* 7729–7730.

Laufer, R., and Wolfe, M. "The Concept of Privacy in Childhood and Adolescence." In D. H. Larson (ed.), *Man-Environment Interactions*. Washington, D.C.: Environmental Design Research Association, 1974.

Lundy, A., and Potts, T. "Recollection of a Transitional Object and Needs for Intimacy and Affiliation in Adolescents." *Psychological Reports*, 1987, *60*, 767–773.

Manosevitz, M., Prentice, N. M., and Wilson, F. "Individual and Family Correlates of Imaginary Companions in Preschool Children." *Developmental Psychology*, 1973, *8*, 72–79.

Masih, V. K. "Imaginary Play Companions of Children." In R. Weizman, R. Brown, P. Levinson, and P. Taylor (eds.), *Piagetian Theory and Its Implications for the Helping Professions*. Vol. 1. Los Angeles: University of Southern California Press, 1978.

Masterson, S. P. "Sex and the Perception of Imaginary Individuals." *Journal of Psychology*, 1975, *91*, 121–126.

Myers, W. A. "Imaginary Companions in Childhood and Adult Creativity." *Psychoanalytic Quarterly*, 1979, *48*, 292–307.

Nagera, H. "The Imaginary Companion: Its Significance for Ego Development and Conflict Solution." *Psychoanalytic Study of the Child*, 1969, *24*, 165–196.

Parker J. G., and Gottman, J. M. "Social and Emotional Development in a Relational Context." In T. J. Berndt and G. W. Ladd (eds.), *Peer Relationships in Child Development*. New York: Wiley, 1989.

Partington, J. T., and Grant, C. "Imaginary Playmates and Other Useful Fantasies." In P. K. Smith (ed.), *Play in Animals and Humans*. Oxford, England: Basil Blackwell, 1984.

Piaget, J. *Play, Dreams, and Imitation in Childhood*. New York: Norton, 1951.

Rivenbark, W. H. "Self-Disclosure Patterns Among Adolescents." *Psychological Reports*, 1971, *28*, 35–42.

Rucker, N. G. "Capacities for Integration, Oedipal Ambivalence, and Imaginary Companions." *American Journal of Psychoanalysis*, 1981, *41*, 129–137.

Savin-Williams, R. C., and Berndt, T. J. "Friendship and Peer Relations." In S. S. Feldman and G. R. Elliott (eds.), *At the Threshold: The Developing Adolescent*. Cambridge, Mass.: Harvard University Press, 1990.

Schaefer, C. E. "Imaginary Companions and Creative Adolescents." *Developmental Psychology*, 1969, *1*, 747–749.

Seiffge-Krenke, I. "Die aktualisierte deutschsprachige Form des OFFER-Self-Concept-Questionnaires" [An updated German-language form of the Offer self-concept questionnaire]. *Zeitschrift für Diagnostik und Differentielle Psychologie*, 1987, *8*, 99–109.

Seiffge-Krenke, I. "Bewältigung alltäglicher Problemsituationen: Ein Coping-Fragebogen für Jugendliche" [Coping with everyday problem situations: A coping questionnaire for adolescents]. *Zeitschrift für Differentielle und Diagnostische Psychologie*, 1989a, *10*, 201–220.

Seiffge-Krenke, I. "Testing the Bereiter Model of Writing: Cognitive and Communicative Aspects of Diary Writing During Adolescence." In H. Mandl, E. de Corte, S. N. Bennett, and H. F. Friedrich (eds.), *Learning and Instruction: European Research in an International Context*. Oxford, England: Pergamon, 1989b.

Seiffge-Krenke, I. *Stress, Coping, and Relationships*. Hillsdale, N.J.: Erlbaum, 1992.

Seiffge-Krenke, I. "Diary Writing in Adolescence: Introspection, Imagination and Creativity." *British Journal of Developmental Psychology*, in press.

Selman, R. L. *The Growth of Interpersonal Understanding: Developmental and Clinical Analyses*. San Diego: Academic Press, 1980.

Sharabany, R., Gershoni, R., and Hofman, J. E. "Girlfriend, Boyfriend: Age and Sex Differences in Intimate Friendship." *Developmental Psychology*, 1981, *17*, 800–808.

Singer, J. L., and Singer, D. G. *Television, Imagination, and Aggression: A Study of Preschoolers*. Hillsdale, N.J.: Erlbaum, 1981.

Sperling, O. E. "An Imaginary Companion, Representing a Prestage of the Superego." *Psychoanalytic Study of the Child*, 1954, *9*, 252–258.

Sroufe, L. A., and Fleeson, J. "Attachment and the Construction of Relationships." In W. W. Hartup and Z. Rubin (eds.), *Relationships and Development*. Hillsdale, N.J.: Erlbaum, 1986.

Sullivan, H. S. *The Interpersonal Theory of Psychiatry*. New York: Norton, 1953.

Svendsen, M. "Children's Imaginary Companions." *Archives of Neurology and Psychiatry*, 1934, *2*, 985–999.

Thompson, C. P. "Diary-Keeping as a Sex-Role Behavior." *Bulletin of the Psychonomic Society*, 1982, *20*, 11–13.

Tobin-Richards, M. H., Boxer, A. M., and Petersen, A. C. "The Psychological Significance of Pubertal Change: Sex Differences in Perceptions of Self During Early Adolescence." In D. Brooks-Gunn and A. C. Petersen (eds.), *Girls at Puberty*. New York: Plenum, 1983.

Westen, D., Klepser, J., Ruffin, S. A., Silverman, M., Litton, N., and Boekamp, J. "Object Relations in Childhood and Adolescence: The Development of Working Representations." *Journal of Consulting and Clinical Psychology*, 1991, *59*, 400–409.

Winnicott, D. W. "Transitional Objects and Transitional Phenomena." *International Journal of Psychoanalysis*, 1953, *34*, 89–97.

Youniss, J., and Smollar, J. *Adolescent Relations with Mothers, Fathers, and Friends*. Chicago: University of Chicago Press, 1985.

INGE SEIFFGE-KRENKE is professor of developmental psychology in the Department of Psychology, University of Bonn, Germany.

*Currently, little attention is paid to theory in the field of adolescent
friendship. Using the chapters in this volume as background, the
author delineates a series of questions that must be addressed by
theorists and empirical investigators alike.*

Theory Is Not a Four-Letter Word:
Needed Directions in the Study
of Adolescent Friendships

Wyndol Furman

The chapters in this volume are welcome additions to the emerging field
of adolescent friendship. Hartup provides a remarkably comprehensive
review of the existing literature on friendships, while the other authors
describe programs of research that have shed new light on these relationships. In this chapter, I use the prior chapters to illustrate themes that are,
or should be, central in the study of adolescent friendship. In particular, I
discuss the state of theory, comparisons with other relationships, variation
within friendships, developmental changes in adolescents and in relationships, the distinction between friendships and friendship networks, the
difference between individual characteristics and relationship characteristics, the role of culture, and process-oriented research.

Although this chapter is intended primarily as a discussion of the
preceding chapters, there is an underlying agenda. Stated simply, theory has
received little attention in the field of adolescent friendship, as is the case in
many other areas in social development. The few theories that exist are
usually not the basis for empirical work. Instead, most investigators (present
company included) simply invoke Harry Stack Sullivan's (1953) theory in an
introductory paragraph, cite a few classic papers documenting the signifi-

Preparation of this chapter was supported by a grant from the National Institute of
Mental Health (BNS 5R01-MH-45830). The research described here was also supported by a W. T. Grant Faculty Scholar Award and a grant from the National Institute
of Child Health and Human Development (RO1HD16142).

cance of friendships, and then proceed with empirical business as usual. As a consequence, we are left with a mass of disparate findings that are difficult to integrate into a coherent whole.

The rationale for theory is well known. Theories propose underlying processes that link different empirical phenomena together. They provide systematic frameworks for understanding friendships and identify important questions for empirical research to examine. Without theory we have little basis for determining what questions are of interest, which study should be done next, and how to approach a question. It is well beyond the scope of this chapter to propose a new theory of friendships, but I delineate a series of conceptual questions that I believe are central to the study of adolescent friendship. Although no single theory can answer all of them, they are questions that a theory should address and that we, as empirical investigators, should keep in mind while planning our research. They can make our work more systematic and thus contribute significantly to the development of our theories.

The State of Theory

The preeminent conceptualization of the field is Sullivan's (1953) interpersonal theory (see Buhrmester and Furman, 1986). Sullivan believed that in preadolescence there is a "need for intimate exchange, for friendship, or for—in its highest refinement—the love of another person, with its enormous facilitation of consensual validation" (1953, p. 291). This need is motivated by the experience of love and the avoidance of loneliness. As this need emerges, a new form of relationship becomes key in social development. Specifically, intimacy is expressed toward a chum or same-sex friend similar in age, background, and interests. Chumships are different from prior types of relationships because they are the first to involve genuine collaboration and to foster the development of social competencies, such as empathy, perspective taking, and altruism. Chumships are also the foundation for adultlike relationships and, in some instances, provide therapeutic experiences that correct prior developmental arrests resulting from difficulties in other relationships.

Sullivan's theory has served as the basis for empirical investigations of differences between children with chumships and those without (for example, Mannarino, 1976; McGuire and Weisz, 1982) and of developmental increases in intimacy (Hunter and Youniss, 1982; Rivenbark, 1971; Sharabany, Gershoni, and Hofman, 1981), although only a few studies have examined the changes that Sullivan predicted between middle childhood and preadolescence (Buhrmester and Furman, 1987; Furman and Buhrmester, 1985). But, overall, the richness of his theory has not yet been fully explored. His proposed links between fulfillment of needs and emotional experiences remain to be tested (see Buhrmester, 1983; Parker and

Asher, in press). The concepts of developmental arrests and therapeutic experiences, as well as their clinical implications, have not been examined. Most important, little attention has been given to the concept of emergent needs or motives. Although this concept has a checkered history, it is hard to imagine a theory of social development without some version of it.

Relatively few theoretical advances have been made since Sullivan's theory. Youniss and his colleagues have integrated Piagetian and Sullivanian ideas into their accounts of adolescents' relationships with parents and peers (Youniss, 1980; Youniss and Smollar, 1985). As they have observed, children are embedded in relationships and are not self-contained thinkers. Children learn from experiences in relationships, which become the frameworks in which meanings of self and other are constructed. Moreover, relationships with parents and peers are structured differently. The reciprocity with peers leads to a different understanding of relationships, one marked by mutuality and the perception of self as a creator of reality. As adolescents reach adulthood, relationships with parents also move in this direction, but peer relationships lead the way. Thus, Youniss and his colleagues have provided a theoretical description of the relative contributions of peer and parent-child relationships to social development.

Recently, a colleague and I proposed a behavioral systems conceptualization of romantic relationships, friendships, and parent-child relationships (Furman and Wehner, in press). Drawing heavily from traditional attachment, adult romantic attachment, and neo-Sullivanian perspectives, we proposed four basic behavioral systems: attachment, caregiving, affiliative, and sexual and reproductive. The first three initially emerge and develop in parent-child relationships. The functioning of the attachment system in infancy, early childhood, and adolescence affects an individual's ability to be attached to another and to provide care. Although the affiliative system first emerges in parent-child relationships, it develops primarily in peer relationships, particularly friendships. Initially, it may simply involve play, but ultimately it develops into a complex system that underlies collaboration, cooperation, coconstruction, and reciprocity in chumships. The sexual and reproductive system emerges at adolescence and is integrated eventually with the other three systems in adult-form romantic relationships.

Experiences with the behavioral systems in other relationships, particularly parent-child relationships, influence views of and experiences in friendships; at the same time, friendships are not mere recreations of other relationships both because of the unique characteristics of friendships and because views of friendships are influenced by experiences with friends. Regardless of how secure adolescents' relationships with parents have been, they are not likely to have secure views of friendships if they have been repeatedly rejected. (Such experiences may, however, be less likely if the parent-child relationship fosters the development of interpersonal skills.) Finally, there are developmental changes in the skill and frequency with which each of the behavior systems are activated in friendships. Although I can only sketch the outlines of this theory here, it presents a series of testable hypotheses about developmental changes, links among relationships, and conscious and automated perceptions of relationships (see Furman and Wehner, in press, for details).

Given the limited number of perspectives now available, it is clear that we must focus more attention on the development of theories of friendships. Moreover, our empirical work would be more systematic and cohesive if we derived our questions from some theory, whether old or new.

Looking Elsewhere for Theory

Fortunately, the investigators in this volume are not guilty of low-altitude empiricism. Instead, their work is based on theoretical frameworks from other areas of social development or social psychology. Bukowski, Hoza, and Boivin's (Chapter Two) approach is derived from self theory, Shulman's (Chapter Four) conceptualization is based on attachment theory and family systems, and Seiffge-Krenke (Chapter Five) draws heavily on psychoanalytic concepts. These conceptualizations have not had widespread application in work on adolescent friendships, but each yields promising insights.

By turning to these theories, we can avoid the pitfalls of developing a separate and isolated field of study with its own theoretical and method-ological frameworks. At the same time, we need to ensure that these theories generalize to friendships. For example, consider Shulman's reliance on fam-ily systems theory. Is it appropriate to think of the peer group as the same type of system as the family unit? Certainly boundaries are more permeable and membership is more fluid in peer groups than in family relationships. Accordingly, the concept of disengaged or enmeshed relationships may have a somewhat different meaning in friendships (as may the sequelae). Simi-larly, we need to consider how the attachment system is manifested in ado-lescent friendships (versus in parent-child relationships in early childhood). Regardless of the answers to these specific questions, the general point is that our conceptual frameworks must be sensitive both to the unique features of friendships and to the features shared with other relationships.

Comparisons Across Relationships

The preceding comments give rise to a general question that must be addressed by any theory: *How and why are friendships similar to and different from other types of personal relationships?* We must answer this question if we are to understand what contributions friendships make to development. That is, we need to specify the distinct properties or processes of friendships that foster developmental advances. The properties or processes that friend-ships share with other relationships are equally important, so our theoretical accounts must be framed in terms of multiple pathways or influences of personal relationships in general.

One way to address the question is to make comparisons across relationships. Several chapters in this volume either explicitly or implicitly do so. For example, Laursen (Chapter Three) compared the frequency and nature of conflict in close peer, parent-child, and other peer and adult relationships. Similarly, Seiffge-Krenke's investigation of imaginary companions entailed comparisons that had not previously been considered. Certainly, imaginary companions and real friends differ on many dimensions, but we may think about imaginary companions as ideal friends and thus glean clues about the desired nature of friendships. Previously, investigators examined children's and adolescents' desires by looking at their conceptions of friendship (for example, Berndt, 1986; Bigelow, 1977; Bigelow and LaGaipa, 1975; Furman and Bierman, 1983, 1984); Seiffge-Krenke's alternative approach is one of the first to directly examine differences between actual and desired or imaginary friendships.

Although no direct comparisons were made, Shulman's family systems approach leads to comparisons. In the original research, Reiss (1981) described three types of family relationships (distance-sensitive, environment-sensitive, and consensus-sensitive), but Shulman only found instances of two. Are there consensus-sensitive friendships? Research suggests that some adolescent romantic relationships can be characterized in this manner (see Furman and Wehner, in press; Shaver and Hazan, in press). Additionally, Sroufe (1991) has reported on friendships with impermeable boundaries. Together, these findings raise questions about what kinds of relationships may be enmeshed and how that enmeshment may be manifested. The answers to these questions will illuminate not only the distinct properties of friendships, but also the processes that are central to friendships.

Other Peer Relationships

What are the similarities and differences between friendships and other peer relationships? Comparisons with other types of peer relationships are particularly important to an understanding of friendships. Comparisons between parent-child relationships and friendships are valuable, but the contrasts are difficult to interpret because of the many differences between the two types of relationships. For example, are dissimilarities due to differences in lengths of the relationships, differences in power structures, the voluntary nature of friendship versus the involuntary nature of parent-child relationships, or something else? By comparing different peer relations, we may be able to rule out some potential explanations.

Bukowski, Hoza, and Boivin implicitly compared features unique to friendship (security and closeness) with those shared with other peer relationships (companionship and help). Other investigators have directly compared interactions with friends to those with acquaintances or strangers (Doyle, Connolly, and Rivest, 1980; Foot, Chapman, and Smith, 1977; Furman, 1987).

Surprisingly few comparisons have been made between friendships and romantic relationships. In fact, virtually no research has been conducted on early or middle adolescents' romantic relationships (Furman and Wehner, in press), although many studies have examined late adolescents' and adults' romantic relationships (Shaver and Hazan, in press; Hendrick and Hendrick, 1992). Most of the research consists of demographic surveys of dating patterns, often done over a decade ago (for example, Hansen, 1977; Wright, 1982). Although adolescent sexuality has recently become a hot topic (see Gullotta, Adams, and Montemayor, 1992; Miller and Moore, 1990), the research has focused on sexual behavior, not on the romantic relationships in which it occurs, relationships that are central in adolescents' social lives.

In the same vein, little is known about opposite-sex friendships. Although these relationships are relatively uncommon in the early school years, they do increase in frequency during adolescence. A few investigators have looked at such relationships (for example, Blyth, Hill, and Thiel, 1982; Sharabany, Gershoni, and Hofman, 1981), but typically without differentiating between platonic and romantic relationships.

The absence of research on adolescent romantic relationships and opposite-sex friendships is ironic in light of Sullivan's (1953) theory of socioemotional development (see Buhrmester and Furman, 1986). The emergence of chumships and the increased need for intimacy, two issues that adolescent friendship researchers have emphasized, first occur in preadolescence. In adolescence, there is an "eruption of true genital interest, felt as lust" (Sullivan, 1953, p. 263). A critical developmental task is learning to balance lust, need for intimacy, and feelings of personal security as one begins to establish relationships with the opposite sex. Clearly, we must give greater attention to these relationships, both in their own right and for the clues that they provide about the nature of friendships in adolescence.

Individual Differences in Friendship

Up to this point, I have emphasized the importance of comparing friendships with other relationships. Equally important, we need to make comparisons among different types of friendships. In effect, we must ask, *How do friendships differ?* Differences in friendship quality may affect adolescents' development and adjustment. Moreover, such variation can provide a rich arena for testing theoretical propositions. For example, if a theory proposes that the intimacy in friendship fosters interpersonal understanding, then adolescents with more intimate friendships should have higher levels of this understanding.

Past investigators have examined developmental differences and sex differences among friends, but relatively few have examined individual differences in friendships. Several authors in this volume, however, address this issue. Shulman presents a family systems typology for classifying friendships, whereas Bukowski, Hoza, and Boivin use a multidimensional framework to describe characteristics of friendships. A number of other investigators have also developed measures of friendship quality (see Furman, in press). Different instruments assess different features, a predictable outcome given the absence of theory to guide methodology. As noted earlier, we as yet have little theoretical or empirical basis for determining which features of friendship are central or how different features are interrelated.

More generally, we need to better understand the underlying structure of friendships. A colleague and I (Adler and Furman, 1988) have proposed that personal relationships, including friendships, can be characterized in terms of four broad dimensions: warmth, conflict, status and power, and comparative features of relationships, such as the exclusivity of friendships. Although existing data fit this model (Adler and Furman, 1988; Furman, in press), it is not yet clear whether these dimensions, particularly power and exclusivity, accurately capture the range of variations among friendships.

When examining variations in friendships, a multivariate approach is essential. Multivariate methods strengthen findings by demonstrating convergences among them. Equally important, the differences found across variables often lead to insights about the phenomena examined. For example, some of the nonsignificant effects in Shulman's work are among his most interesting findings. Although they differed in reasoning about friendships, disengaged and interdependent pairs did not differ in the nature, location, or frequency of joint activities. This pattern of findings suggests that the difference between the two types is not simply one of satisfactory versus unsatisfactory relationships. Instead, the two seem to differ in terms of intimacy or attachment, not affiliation. Testing of such differential patterns leads to more precise explanations.

Shulman's typological approach also raises the question of whether there are different kinds of friendships. For example, perhaps same-sex and opposite-sex friendships constitute different categories of personal relationships. Similarly, it is not clear if best friendships are qualitatively different from other friendships or are simply more intense versions of the same type of relationship. Moreover, we need to determine whether a typological or dimensional approach is useful for describing individual variation in a particular kind of friendship. Clearly, such assessments require a theoretical rationale as well as an empirical basis.

Although recent efforts to examine individual differences in friendship quality are important, this factor is not the only source of variation in friendships. Adolescents also vary in *who* their friends are. Hartup (Chapter One) reviews a number of studies demonstrating that the identities of one's friends are also important. If we are to conceptualize and study the influence of friendships, we need to take both the characteristics of friends and the characteristics of the friendships into account simultaneously (for example, Berndt and Keefe, 1992); moreover, our models must illuminate how characteristics of friends influence friendships. These complications not-withstanding, the emphasis on the quality of friendships is a promising new direction.

Developmental Differences

To understand developmental differences, we need to ask, *How and why do friendships change as adolescents develop?* Any adequate theoretical account of friendships must address developmental change. In the present volume, Seiffge-Krenke describes age trends in imaginary companions, and Shulman reports age differences in friendship typologies. Other investigators have also found age-related changes in the intimacy of friendships (see Hartup, this volume). Yet we have only begun to scratch the surface of this issue. There may be differences not only in the levels of various characteristics but also in the patterns of relations within (that is, the underlying structure) and across variables (see Connell and Furman, 1984). Aside from research demonstrating developmental differences in links between intimacy and interpersonal competence (Buhrmester, 1990), these types of changes have received little attention, conceptually or empirically.

Shulman's findings highlight a particularly intriguing problem. Early adolescents tended to establish disengaged friendships, whereas middle ad-olescents favored interdependent friendships. Do differences among adoles-cents of a particular age group reflect differences in developmental status or some other source of individual differences? In other words, do early adolescents with disengaged friendships eventually develop interdependent friendships? Longitudinal work is necessary to determine whether some adolescents are on a different developmental trajectory or are simply "delayed." The two alternatives are quite distinct conceptually. Further theoretical and empirical consideration must be given to developmental differences if we are to better understand the significance of different characteristics at different ages.

Temporal Changes in Friendships

Just as adolescents develop, so also do their relationships (Furman, 1984b). Friendships are initiated, maintained, and eventually dissolved. Thus, we need to ask, *How and why do friendships change over the course of their existence?* Simple comparisons among friendships or with other relation-ships cannot capture the dynamic processes that are involved in develop-ment. By examining changes within a relationship, we can test theoretical propositions about the impact of certain characteristics or processes on individuals and their relationships. Moreover, a temporal perspective enriches our conceptualization of relationships.

Early theories of interpersonal attraction focused on the role of static characteristics of individuals, such as physical attraction. A temporal perspective leads us to expect the influence of these characteristics to change over the course of relationship development. Moreover, dynamic properties that emerge with the development of a relationship may shape the future course of the relationship (see Furman, 1984b).

In the present volume, Laursen's assessment of the impact of conflicts on relationships and Shulman's examination of reasons for terminating friendships are illustrations of the kind of research that is needed to understand temporal changes. Hartup reviews additional studies on the dissolution of friendships; still, the topic warrants greater conceptual and empirical attention.

Friendships and Friendship Networks

Adolescents vary in the numbers of their friendships. Some have none, whereas many have several. Accordingly, we must distinguish between a friendship and a network of friendships (or, as Hartup expresses the contrast, "my best friend" versus "my friends"). We need to ask, *How can we characterize friendship networks and their influence?*

Certainly, we need to know the number of friendships that an adolescent has established, the identities of these friends, and the quality of the relationships (Bukowski and Hoza, 1989; Hartup, this volume), but this information may not be sufficient or the right conceptual metric for describing a network of friendships. For example, consider three adolescents: The first does not have any friends, the second has one best friend and three other friends, and the third has ten friends but no best friends. Of course, the identity of these friends and the qualitative features of all of the relationships are likely to vary as well. How do we describe the differences among these adolescents? Which relationship gets compared to which? Do we average the scores of different relationships to control for differences in the number of relationships? Do we use the "closest" friendships? Do we eliminate the adolescent without friends, thus reducing a significant proportion of the variance in the sample? These are the kinds of questions that researchers face when describing the diverse structures of contemporary families. Hartup rightly points out that we lack the theoretical models needed to account for the influences of "best friends" and "my friends" and the interface between the two.

Popularity or peer status must also be considered. For years, investigators studying younger children's peer relations focused almost exclusively on sociometric status, giving little attention to the role of friendship. Only recently have investigators recognized that the two differ both conceptually and empirically (see Bukowski and Hoza, 1989; Furman and Robbins, 1985). Friendship theorists and researchers must not replicate this error by excluding peer status variables in their investigations.

The measurement of popularity and other peer group variables with adolescent subjects presents thorny conceptual and methodological problems. Although it is reasonable to assume that classmates or grademates are peers during the elementary school years, the concept of a single peer reference group is less plausible in the context of secondary schools, where peer cliques are more salient and peer population groupings are larger in size and more fluid. This problem is compounded by the possibility that likability and popularity become more distinct as adolescents grow older. Future investigators must make inroads into these knotty problems.

Individual Characteristics and Friendship Characteristics

Another critical question is, *How are individual characteristics and friendship characteristics related?* For both theoretical and applied reasons, we are interested in understanding not just friendships but also adolescents.

Several of the authors in this volume provide relevant empirical data. For example, Bukowski, Hoza, and Boivin examined links between friendship and perceived competence, whereas Shulman looked at ties between type of friendship and social-cognitive variables. In each of these cases (and in most instances in the literature), however, the investigators only looked at the characteristics of single individuals. Friendships, like other relationships, are dyadic phenomena, influenced by the characteristics of both individuals as well as by the interaction or meshing of these characteristics (see Furman, 1984a). When we examine only the characteristics of single individuals, correlations between individuals and friendships are necessarily limited. Given this limitation, the documented links of friendship with self-esteem and social cognition are particularly impressive.

Not only are there limitations in our derivation of relationship characteristics from a particular individual's characteristics, but, vice versa, there are also limitations in our ability to identify an individual's interpersonal competence from the characteristics of his or her relationships. A disturbed or unsatisfactory friendship does not necessarily mean that a particular adolescent has an interpersonal difficulty. Perhaps the partner is the source of the difficulty or perhaps the relational problems reflect a poor meshing of the two individuals' characteristics.

How then can we infer individual characteristics from relationship characteristics? One solution is to control the input of the other with a standardized role-playing or structured task. It is not clear, however, whether individuals interact in the same manner during such tasks as they do in more naturalistic settings (see Furman, 1984a). Moreover, standardization may distort the typical course of social interactions. A socially incompetent person may elicit responses different from those elicited by a socially competent person, which may in turn affect the behavior of the partner (Snyder, Tanke, and Berscheid, 1977). Thus, standardization of responses may make interactions artificial and underestimate differences between a socially competent and an incompetent person. But it may also exaggerate differences because in natural settings partners may compensate for ineffectual behaviors. For example, when interacting with someone who is withdrawn or reticent, an adolescent may compensate by talking more than usual. If the partner's response is standardized to a fixed length, the interaction may be more stilted than would be the case in a natural setting.

An alternative solution is to look for patterns across different friendships. If consistencies are observed, inferences about interpersonal characteristics may be stronger. But even this approach presents problems. In particular, it is not clear if such patterns reflect a person's interpersonal proclivities or the kinds of people with whom he or she develops friendships. Although both possibilities say something about the individual, the theoretical and applied implications are quite different.

These conceptual problems are compounded by the fact that a relationship is influenced not only by the characteristics of the two individuals and the meshing of such characteristics but also by the history of the relationship. That is, the individuals' past experiences and expectations for the future influence the nature of their relationship. Certainly, past experiences and expectations are influenced by the participants' characteristics, but they are also influenced by situational factors and chance occurrences (Bandura, 1982). After all, if we were to recall the history of one of our own friendships or romantic relationships, could we completely account for the course of the relationship by knowing who was involved? The role of relationship histories must be incorporated into our conceptualizations of friendship.

These difficulties are all relevant to developmental psychologists. As Hartup observes, the search for continuities across relationships is an intriguing task for researchers. If relationships are influenced by their histories and partner characteristics, the task of identifying continuities is seriously complicated. A friendship may be linked with parent-child relationships, but it is also strongly influenced by past experiences in that relationship or that type of relationship (Furman and Wehner, in press). The idea that current relationships are mere recapitulations of past relationships is too simplistic.

In sum, relationship characteristics and individual characteristics constitute two fundamentally different levels of analysis. As we develop theoretical frameworks or conduct empirical studies, we need to be clear about whether we are studying adolescents or friendships. Efforts to link the two are exciting, but many conceptual and methodological problems must be addressed if our efforts are to be successful (see Furman, 1984a).

Friendships and Culture

In addition to questions about the links between individual and relationship characteristics, we may also want to ask, *How does culture influence friendship?* Identification of cultural differences may give us clues about which features of friendships are universal and which vary by culture. Moreover, studies of the influence of friendships in different cultures, just like studies of individual variations in friendships, can test theoretical propositions. Certainly, we want our theories to account for more than white, middle-class friendships.

Although the empirical studies described in this volume were conducted in four different countries, the issue of cultural influences was not addressed. Comparisons among Israeli, German, and North American infants are of particular interest in the literature on attachment theory (see van IJzendorn, 1990). Also, Brain (1987) describes marked cultural differences in friendships and romantic relationships. Certainly, Hartup's description of the literature on demographic homophilies suggests that differences are likely to emerge, though few psychological studies have examined them (for example, DeRosier and Kupersmidt, 1991; Steinberg, Dornbusch, and Brown, 1992). In fact, as Hartup observes, most of the research focuses on Caucasian children and adolescents. Clearly, cultural influences warrant more attention.

A Brief Note on Process

Finally, we need to ask, *What processes underlie friendships and their influence?* One of the most impressive features of the chapters in this volume is that they tell us as much about social processes as they do about friendships. For example, self-esteem researchers will be interested in Bukowski, Hoza, and Boivin's findings, those who study identity development will want to examine Seiffge-Krenke's work, and those who study the development of social cognition will benefit from Shulman's research.

Laursen's work exemplifies the intermeshing of process and relationship research. In his empirical study, a number of differences in conflict among relationships were identified. He also discusses how the processes of conflict and conflict management vary as a function of relationship closeness, reciprocity, and interests and activities. Years ago, investigators studying social learning processes paid little attention to relational context. That is, in examining imitation, aggression, or prosocial behavior, they were not concerned with how behaviors, processes, and underlying meanings differ as a function of the relationship context. With the increased focus on relationships, we should not make the same kind of mistake by neglecting the processes underlying these relationships. The study of processes is particularly important for the development of theory. After all, we want not only to describe friendships but also to understand what makes them tick, how they develop, and how they influence adolescents.

Conclusion

In discussing the chapters in this volume, I have posed nine key questions: How and why are friendships similar to and different from other personal relationships? What are the similarities and differences between friendships and other peer relationships? How do friendships differ? How and why do friendships change as adolescents develop? How and why do friendships change over the course of their existence? How can we characterize friendship networks and their influence? How are individual characteristics and friendship characteristics related? How does culture influence friendship? And what processes underlie friendships and their influence? Although this list is not complete, a comprehensive theory of adolescent friendships must address these issues. If we reexamine the theories described earlier, we can see that while different questions are addressed by different theories, no one theory addresses all of them. Consideration of these questions can only enrich all of our conceptualizations of friendships.

These issues are equally relevant to the garden variety empirical investigator. The variables that we select, the measures and methods that we use, and the questions that we ask are always grounded in some theory, even if it is only implicit. If we consider conceptual implications as we design our empirical work, we can make greater progress in theory development. After all, theory is not a four-letter word.

References

Adler, T., and Furman, W. "A Model for Close Relationships and Relationship Dysfunctions." In S. W. Duck (ed.), *Handbook of Personal Relationships: Theory, Research and Interventions*. London: Wiley, 1988.

Bandura, A. "The Psychology of Chance Encounters and Life Patterns." *American Psychologist*, 1982, *37*, 747–755.

Berndt, T. J. "Children's Comments About Their Friendships." In M. Perlmutter (ed.), *Cognitive Perspectives on Children's Social and Behavioral Development*. Hillsdale, N.J.: Erlbaum, 1986.

Berndt, T. J., and Keefe, K. "Influences of Friends' Characteristics and Friendship Features on Adolescents' Behavior and Adjustment." Unpublished manuscript, Department of Psychology, Purdue University, 1992.

Bigelow, B. J. "Children's Friendship Expectations: A Cognitive-Developmental Study." *Child Development*, 1977, *48*, 247–253.

Bigelow, B. J., and LaGaipa, J. J. "Children's Written Descriptions of Friendship: A Multidimensional Analysis." *Developmental Psychology*, 1975, *11*, 857–858.

Blyth, D. A., Hill, J. P., and Thiel, K. S. "Early Adolescents' Significant Others: Grade and Gender Differences in Perceived Relationships with Familial and Nonfamilial Adults and Young People." *Journal of Youth and Adolescence*, 1982, *11*, 425–449.

Brain, R. *Friends and Lovers*. New York: Basic Books, 1987.

Buhrmester, D. "Toward a Model of Socioemotional Development in Preadolescence and Adolescence." Unpublished doctoral dissertation, Department of Psychology, University of Denver, 1983.

Buhrmester, D. "Intimacy of Friendship, Interpersonal Competence, and Adjustment in Preadolescence and Adolescence." *Child Development*, 1990, *61*, 1101–1111.

Buhrmester, D., and Furman, W. "The Changing Functions of Friends in Childhood: A Neo-Sullivanian Perspective." In V. G. Derlega and B. A. Winstead (eds.), *Friendship and Social Interaction*. New York: Springer-Verlag, 1986.

Buhrmester, D., and Furman, W. "The Development of Companionship and Intimacy." *Child Development*, 1987, *58*, 1101–1113.

Bukowski, W. M., and Hoza, B. "Popularity and Friendship: Issues in Theory, Measurement, and Outcome." In T. J. Berndt and G. W. Ladd (eds.), *Peer Relationships in Child Development*. New York: Wiley, 1989.

Connell, J. C., and Furman, W. "Conceptual and Methodological Issues in the Study of Transitions." In R. Harmon and R. Emde (eds.), *Continuity and Discontinuity in Development*. New York: Plenum, 1984.

DeRosier, M. E., and Kupersmidt, J. B. "Costa Rican Children's Perceptions of Their Social Networks." *Developmental Psychology*, 1991, *27*, 656–662.

Doyle, A., Connolly, J. K., and Rivest, L. "The Effect of Playmate Familiarity on the Social Interactions of Young Children." *Child Development*, 1980, *51*, 217–223.

Foot, H. C., Chapman, A. J., and Smith, J. R. "Friendship and Social Responsiveness in Boys and Girls." *Journal of Personality and Social Psychology*, 1977, *35*, 401–411.

Furman, W. "Issues in the Assessment of Social Skills of Normal and Handicapped Children." In T. Field, M. Siegal, and J. L. Roopnarine (eds.), *Friendships of Normal and Handicapped Children*. Norwood, N.J.: Ablex, 1984a.

Furman, W. "Some Observations on the Study of Personal Relationships." In J. C. Masters and K. Yarkin-Levin (eds.), *Interfaces Between Developmental and Social Psychology*. San Diego: Academic Press, 1984b.

Furman, W. "Acquaintanceship in Middle Childhood." *Developmental Psychology*, 1987, *23*, 563–570.

Furman, W. "The Measurement of Children's and Adolescents' Perceptions of Friendships: Conceptual and Methodological Issues." In W. M. Bukowski, A. F. Newcomb, and W. W. Hartup (eds.), *The Company They Keep: Friendships in Childhood and Adolescence*. New York: Cambridge University Press, in press.

Furman, W., and Bierman, K. L. "Developmental Changes in Young Children's Conceptions of Friendship." *Child Development*, 1983, *54*, 549–556.

Furman, W., and Bierman, K. L. "Children's Conceptions of Friendship: A Multimethod Study of Developmental Changes." *Developmental Psychology*, 1984, *20*, 925–931.

Furman, W., and Buhrmester, D. "Children's Perceptions of the Personal Relationships in Their Social Networks." *Developmental Psychology*, 1985, *21*, 1016–1024.

Furman, W., and Robbins, P. "What's the Point? Issues in the Selection of Treatment Objectives." In B. H. Schneider, K. H. Rubin, and J. E. Ledingham (eds.), *Children's Peer Relations: Issues in Assessment and Intervention*. New York: Springer-Verlag, 1985.

Furman, W., and Wehner, E. A. "Romantic Views: Toward a Theory of Adolescent Romantic Relationships." In R. Montemayor (ed.), *Relationships in Adolescence*. Newbury Park, Calif.: Sage, in press.

Gullotta, T. P., Adams, G. R., and Montemayor, R. (eds.). *Adolescent Sexuality*. Newbury Park, Calif.: Sage, 1992.

Hansen, S. L. "Dating Choices of High School Students." *Family Coordinator,* 1977, *26,* 133–138.

Hendrick, S. S., and Hendrick, C. *Romantic Love.* Newbury Park, Calif.: Sage, 1992.

Hunter, F. T., and Youniss, J. "Changes in Functions of Three Relations During Adolescence." *Developmental Psychology,* 1982, *18,* 806–811.

McGuire, K. D., and Weisz, J. R. "Social Cognition and Behavior Correlates of Preadolescent Chumship." *Child Development,* 1982, *53,* 1478–1484.

Mannarino, A. P. "Friendship Patterns and Altruistic Behavior in Preadolescent Males." *Developmental Psychology,* 1976, *12,* 555–556.

Miller, B. C., and Moore, K. A. "Adolescent Sexual Behavior, Pregnancy, and Parenting: Research Through the 1980s." *Journal of Marriage and the Family,* 1990, *52,* 1025–1044.

Parker, J. G., and Asher, S. R. "Friendship and Friendship Quality in Middle Childhood: Links with Peer Group Acceptance and Feelings of Loneliness and Social Dissatisfaction." *Developmental Psychology,* in press.

Reiss, D. *The Family's Construction of Reality.* Cambridge, Mass.: Harvard University Press, 1981.

Rivenbark, W. H. "Self-Disclosure Patterns Among Adolescents." *Psychological Reports,* 1971, *28,* 35–42.

Sharabany, R., Gershoni, R., and Hofman, J. E. "Girlfriend, Boyfriend: Age and Sex Differences in Intimate Friendship." *Developmental Psychology,* 1981, *17,* 800–808.

Shaver, P. R., and Hazan, C. "Adult Romantic Attachment: Theory and Evidence." In D. Perlman and W. Jones (eds.), *Advances in Personal Relationships.* Vol. 4. Greenwich, Conn.: JAI, in press.

Snyder, M., Tanke, E. D., and Berscheid, E. "Social Perception and Interpersonal Behavior: On the Self-Fulfilling Nature of Social Stereotypes." *Journal of Personality and Social Psychology,* 1977, *35,* 656–666.

Sroufe, L. A. "Models of Relationships and Quality of Friendships in Pre-Adolescence: Links to Attachment History and Preschool Social Competence." Paper presented at the biennial meeting of the Society for Research in Child Development, Seattle, Apr. 1991.

Steinberg, L., Dornbusch, S. M., and Brown, B. B. "Ethnic Differences in Adolescent Achievement: An Ecological Perspective." *American Psychologist,* 1992, *47,* 723–729.

Sullivan, H. S. *The Interpersonal Theory of Psychiatry.* New York: Norton, 1953.

Van IJzendorn, M. H. (ed.). "Cross-Cultural Validity of Attachment Theory." *Human Development,* 1990, *33* (entire issue 1).

Wright, L. S. "Parental Permission to Date and Its Relationship to Drug Use and Suicidal Thought Among Adolescents." *Adolescence,* 1982, *17,* 409–418.

Youniss, J. *Parents and Peers in Social Development: A Piaget-Sullivan Perspective.* Chicago: University of Chicago Press, 1980.

Youniss, J., and Smollar, J. *Adolescent Relations with Mothers, Fathers, and Friends.* Chicago: University of Chicago Press, 1985.

WYNDOL FURMAN is professor in the Department of Psychology, University of Denver, and director of the Relationship Center.

INDEX

ORDERING INFORMATION

NEW DIRECTIONS FOR CHILD DEVELOPMENT is a series of paperback books that presents the latest research findings on all aspects of children's psychological development, including their cognitive, social, moral, and emotional growth. Books in the series are published quarterly in fall, winter, spring, and summer and are available for purchase by subscription and individually.

SUBSCRIPTIONS for 1993 cost $52.00 for individuals (a savings of 25 percent over single-copy prices) and $70.00 for institutions, agencies, and libraries. Please do not send institutional checks for personal subscriptions. Standing orders are accepted.

SINGLE COPIES cost $17.95 when payment accompanies order. (California, New Jersey, New York, and Washington, D.C., residents please include appropriate sales tax.) Billed orders will be charged postage and handling.

DISCOUNTS for quantity orders are available. Please write to the address below for information.

ALL ORDERS must include either the name of an individual or an official purchase order number. Please submit your order as follows:
   Subscriptions: specify series and year subscription is to begin
   Single copies: include individual title code (such as CD1)

MAIL ALL ORDERS TO:
   Jossey-Bass Publishers
   350 Sansome Street
   San Francisco, California 94104

FOR SINGLE-COPY SALES OUTSIDE OF THE UNITED STATES CONTACT:
   Maxwell MacMillan International Publishing Group
   866 Third Avenue
   New York, New York 10022

FOR SUBSCRIPTION SALES OUTSIDE OF THE UNITED STATES, contact any international subscription agency or Jossey-Bass directly.

OTHER TITLES AVAILABLE IN THE
NEW DIRECTIONS FOR CHILD DEVELOPMENT SERIES
William Damon, Editor-in-Chief